W9-AWK-379

SCHOLASTIC

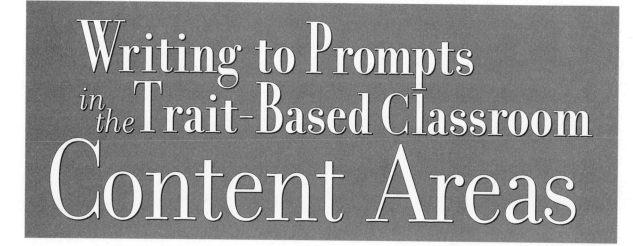

Writing to Prompts in the Trait-Based Classroom Content Areas

Prompts That Provide All the Elements Students Need to Start Writing:
A *Role*, *Audience*, *Format*, *Topic*, and *Strong Verb* (R.A.F.T.S.)

by Ruth Culham & Amanda Wheeler

NEW YORK • TORONTO • LONDON • AUCKLAND • SYDNEY
MEXICO CITY • NEW DELHI • HONG KONG • BUENOS AIRES

Teaching *Resources*

DEDICATION

To my family members, who continue to love and support me through life's many seasons —rc

To dedicated teachers everywhere who inspire and encourage students each and every day —aw

ACKNOWLEDGMENT

As teachers across the country participate in the National Writing Projects, they share ideas for teaching students about writing. The seed for this book was planted through the Montana Writing Project and the early, groundbreaking work of Nancy Vendeventer, a former teacher in Bozeman, Montana, in 1979. This text is an extension of that work and a reflection of how extensively this strategy for inspiring writers and writing has been integrated into the everyday life of teachers and students.

Many thanks to the teachers, administrators, and staff developers across the country who nagged us mercilessly for this book. Without your ideas, encouragement, and enthusiasm, this text would never have come to pass. We hope it lives up to your expectations and becomes a staple in your classrooms and schools.

Scholastic Inc. grants teachers permission to photocopy the reproducible pages of this book for classroom use only. No other part of this publication may be reproduced in whole or in part, or stored in a retrieval system, or transmitted in any form or by any means, electronic, mechanical, photocopying, recording, or otherwise, without written permission of the publisher.
For information regarding permission, write to
Scholastic Inc., 557 Broadway, New York, NY 10012.

Cover design by Maria Lilja
Interior design by Holly Grundon
Photograph by Tom Hurst via SODA

ISBN 0-439-55685-6
Copyright © 2003 by The Writing Traits Company
All rights reserved. Published by Scholastic Inc.
Printed in the U.S.A.

3 4 5 6 7 8 9 10   40   09 08 07 06 05 04

Contents

Introduction

Getting students to write and keeping them writing is a challenge. Typically, they need help learning how to narrow their topics so they are manageable, how to organize their ideas so they fit their purpose for the writing, and how to use specific language that brings their ideas to life. R.A.F.T.S. can help. They help students start writing with focus, clarity, and energy.

What Are R.A.F.T.S. Prompts?

R.A.F.T.S., a classroom-tested technique for creating focused writing prompts, was first shared by Nancy Vendeventer, a talented teacher from Bozeman, Montana. Each prompt provides students with the baseline information they need to focus their writing:

- a *Role* from which to write

- an *Audience* to address

- a *Format* in which to write

- a *Topic* about which to write

- a *Strong verb* that suggests the purpose of the writing

Structured but not rigid, this format gives students the mental elbow room to write interesting, original pieces.

In this book, you will find over 75 ready-to-use R.A.F.T.S. prompts on content area topics, plus ideas for creating your own R.A.F.T.S. The prompts for math and science are based on standards designed by the National Council of Teachers of Mathematics and the National Academy of Sciences. The prompts for social studies are based on thematic strands from the National Council for the Social Studies. We've included a mixture of topics that appeal to boys and girls, and address contemporary, real-life situations such as deciding the best way to approach a problem and understanding the impact of current events. There's plenty of material to get your students started writing in the content areas.

How Are R.A.F.T.S. Prompts Constructed?

Constructing a R.A.F.T.S. prompt is simple:

- First, identify each component of the prompt. For example, if your students are studying endangered animals and the impact of human encroachment on their environments, you might choose these components:

Role:	endangered flying squirrel
Audience:	construction company president
Format:	letter
Topic:	find someplace else to build and leave your forest alone
Strong Verb:	persuade

- Next, write the prompt in paragraph form. Since establishing a role for the writer is the first step, most R.A.F.T.S. prompts start with "You are…":

  You are an endangered flying squirrel living in a forest that is about to be leveled to make way for a shopping center. Write a letter to the construction company president persuading him to find someplace else to build and leave your forest alone.

- Then, underline and label the key components of the prompt to ensure that students have all of the necessary pieces to make their writing work:

  Imagine you are an <u>endangered flying squirrel</u> living in a forest
  (Role)
  that is about to be leveled to make way for a shopping center.

  Write a <u>letter</u> to the <u>construction company president</u> <u>persuading</u> him
  (Format)   (Audience)   (Strong verb)
  to <u>find someplace else to build and leave your forest alone</u>.
  (Topic)

- Last, introduce the R.A.F.T.S. prompt to students by identifying the purpose for each component and then provide enough time for them to create successful pieces. (For more information on introducing R.A.F.T.S., see pages 8–10 and 13–16.)

Dear Construction Company President,

I am an endangered flying squirrel and part of a very large family currently living in the Southwest Forest. This is the same Southwest Forest that your company plans to clear to build a shopping center.

Shopping centers may be good for humans but they aren't so good for endangered flying squirrels. Generations of flying squirrels have called this forest home for hundreds of years. If you clear our trees, where will we go? How will we find food? We will surely die out. I am wondering, is this shopping center worth the extinction of our species?

In order to have a part in protecting our species, maybe you could put your shopping center someplace else. You might want to think about that old vacant lot next to the game arcade. Don't you think that parents would love to shop while their children are playing games?

My family and I hope you will do the right thing to save our species, and allow us to live in our forest forever.

Sincerely,

Rocky

R.A.F.T.S. prompts give students just the right amount of structure along with freedom to be creative—a great combination for writing success! This book places ready-to-use literature-based prompts at your fingertips, and provides quick, easy guidelines for creating and using your own prompts.

What Are the Benefits of Using R.A.F.T.S. Prompts?

There are many benefits to using R.A.F.T.S. Here, we focus on three: Helping students gain content knowledge, helping them understand and apply writing traits, and helping them become proficient in the writing modes.

R.A.F.T.S. PROMPTS HELP STUDENTS GAIN CONTENT KNOWLEDGE

In his book *Writing to Learn*, William Zinsser explains, "Writing across the curriculum isn't just a method of getting students to write who are afraid of writing. It is also a method of getting students to learn what they were afraid of learning." Whether they are investigating life forms at the deepest depths of the ocean, designing a new playground scheme, or observing the mating habits of the New Zealand kiwi, students need to write it all down to make sense of what they find out through questioning and research. Writing allows them the freedom to explore what they care about, where their passions lie.

Of course, exposing students to models of good writing is always a smart thing to do—and we have so many fine published works from which to draw. In social studies, for example, students have glorious historical documents such as "The Declaration of Independence" and "The Gettysburg Address," intriguing political essays by Ellen Goodman or William Safire, and lively texts from contemporary humorists such as Dave Barry or Garrison Keillor that serve as excellent models of good writing and help students make connections from their world at school to the outside world. Science teachers have a plethora of fine writing texts at their disposal to use as models for students, too, from Carl Sagan's books on space exploration and David Quammen's essays on natural history, to Robert Pollack's fascinating work *Signs of Life: The Language and Meanings of DNA*. Math teachers can draw from published essays, journals, and even stories to share with students as models of what good writing in math class looks like. Greg Tang's picture books, *The Grapes of Math* and *Math for All Seasons*, are sure to delight students with their content and uproarious style. Algebra students will always remember *The Number Devil: A Mathematical Adventure* by Hans Magnus Enzensberger.

Writing in the content areas can further students' zest for learning. It is the bridge between the questions students have and the answers they find as they delve deeply into what Ralph Fletcher calls "fierce wonderings." First they ask the questions that need answering about a topic, then they gather information, then they write. It is this writing that is finalized into a form that is shareable. R.A.F.T.S. prompts provide a flexible structure for students as they prepare their ideas—all kinds of ideas—to be read and appreciated by readers.

Writing is not something we do simply in response to literature. We write to make sense of our world; we write to understand how things work; we write to figure things out. The R.A.F.T.S. prompts in this book are designed to help you tap into topics that are meaningful to students, and to allow students to write about what they know. That's the secret. These prompts help students not only to become better writers, but to become better thinkers.

Learning to write? Writing to learn? It all happens when students write. Writing will fill students' minds and bodies with the very stuff that will nourish them for a lifetime.

R.A.F.T.S. PROMPTS HELP STUDENTS UNDERSTAND AND APPLY WRITING TRAITS

R.A.F.T.S. prompts go hand-in-hand with the traits of writing. In the mid-1980's, a group of teachers from districts across the country realized they needed a reliable and accurate tool to measure student writing performance. By reading and sorting stacks of student writing into "good," "fair," and "poor" categories and then analyzing that writing closely, they identified characteristics that were common to all the pieces. What resulted from their efforts ultimately became an analytic assessment model that identifies seven key characteristics, or traits, of writing:

- **Ideas:** the meaning and development of the message

- **Organization:** the internal structure of the piece

- **Voice:** the way the writer brings the topic to life

- **Word Choice:** the specific vocabulary the writer uses to convey meaning

- **Sentence Fluency:** the way the words and phrases flow throughout the text

- **Conventions:** the mechanical correctness of the piece

- **Presentation:** the overall appearance of the work

When writing to a R.A.F.T.S. prompt, students focus on traits. Specifically:

- **Role** and **Audience** help students decide on the **voice** and **word choice**.

- **Format** helps students with the **organization** of the writing.

- **Topic** helps students zero in on the **ideas** of the writing.

- **Strong Verbs** direct students to the writing purpose (e.g. "persuade," "analyze," "predict," and "compare") and, from there, help them to write clearly using all the traits: **ideas, organization, voice, word choice, sentence fluency, conventions,** and **presentation**.

When students compose with the traits in mind, they find writing much more manageable. They work with these traits throughout the writing process, as they prewrite, draft, revise, edit, and prepare a final copy. For example, the traits help them plan their writing and ask themselves important questions as they write, such as: "Will my idea make sense to the reader? Is all the information in the right place or should I move some things around? Who am I writing to and is this the right voice to use for this audience? Are my words interesting, accurate, and precise? Do my sentences make sense and flow as the piece is read? Have I edited for spelling, capitals, grammar, paragraphing, and punctuation? Does my writing have a polished, finished look?"

Students can apply the traits in the writing they do in all of their classes, not just English class. Whether it's a math problem to be solved, a social studies research project, or a science laboratory report, the traits of writing will help students express their ideas clearly. And, using the language of the traits as the foundation, R.A.F.T.S. becomes a tool for you to use to help students. By combining instruction in the traits with R.A.F.T.S. prompts, you give students everything they need to generate interesting, original, and finely crafted writing.

What You Should Know and What You Might Tell Students About R.A.F.T.S.

Once you have chosen a R.A.F.T.S. prompt, introduce it to students. Start by defining each component and sharing how it links to the traits of writing. The chart on the next two pages contains ideas and language to help you get started. Once students understand how the R.A.F.T.S. components can help them focus their writing, use the prompts in this book and watch your students' writing soar!

ROLE

The **R**ole of the writer is as varied as your imagination. Roles can be gleaned from subject-area topics, school situations, book characters, and real people—the sky's the limit. When the student assumes a role other than him- or herself, he or she must decide on the appropriate voice for the piece. When introducing the **R**ole, remind students that the **R**ole asks them to think about **Who is the author of this piece?**

Think about the way this author would write about the topic. What voice is just right for this piece of writing? Exuberant? Edgy? Confident? Hilarious? Serious? Considerate? The words and phrases in your writing should enhance the voice you choose. Ask yourself, "How would this person use words to express him- or herself clearly and make his or her voice heard?"

AUDIENCE

You, the teacher, are your students' typical **A**udience. By assigning a specific **A**udience, you can empower students to communicate their ideas to someone other than yourself. Encourage them to think about how best to reach their audience through voice and word choice, making sure to consider what they know about the topic. When introducing **A**udience to students, have them place themselves in the assigned **R**ole, then answer the question, **Who is the audience for this writing?**

When writing to a certain **A**udience, keep in mind that you will need to determine the perfect match of voice and word choice to communicate your ideas. Consider the relationship between the role and the audience and the kind of voice that is most appropriate. Think about the words you will use. Should you be formal? Informal? What vocabulary should be explained? Be sure to think about not only *what* needs to be said, but also *how* it needs to be said to address a particular **A**udience.

FORMAT

Assigning a specific **F**ormat gives you the opportunity to help students learn about many possible organizational structures for their writing. (See "Formats and Strong Verbs to Consider When Creating Your Own Prompts," page 80.) Teach them to write brochures, directions, advertisements, letters, and so forth. By learning different **F**ormats, students will practice organizing their ideas in many different ways. When introducing **F**ormat to students, have them think about the question **How do the ideas need to be organized?**

There are many different formats for writing. By focusing on **F**ormat, you will be practicing and learning organizational structures for your writing. Once you know the format for the piece you are going to write, ask yourself, "How do I organize this piece to achieve this particular **F**ormat? Where should it start? What goes in the middle? How will it end? What should my writing look like? What are the most important organizational issues when I write in this format?"

Writing to Prompts in the Trait-Based Classroom: Content Areas Scholastic Teaching Resources

TOPIC

The Topic helps students focus on the details of their writing so that their ideas develop as clearly as possible. The Topic should be well defined and contain clear guidelines such as: "Write a persuasive letter to the city planner and include several strong arguments for a new public swimming pool in your area." Giving students these clear guidelines helps them determine how much information they should include in order to develop their ideas fully. When introducing the Topic to students, have them think about the question, **What is the main idea of the writing?**

If the Topic of your writing is to explain or inform the reader of something, ask yourself, "Have I included enough information so that the reader thinks I'm an expert?" "Do all my ideas add up to something important?" "Have I told the reader something he or she doesn't already know?" If the topic is to develop a narrative, ask yourself, "Is my story fully developed and complete?" "Have I written a story that is interesting and will hold the reader's attention?" "Have I put in just the right amount of detail?"

STRONG VERB

A Strong Verb, such as *persuade*, *analyze*, *create*, *predict*, or *compare*, helps students see the purpose of the writing and, from there, determine the appropriate ideas, organization, voice, word choice, sentence fluency, and conventions for their writing. (See "Formats and Strong Verbs to Consider When Creating Your Own Prompts," page 80.) Help students see how being clear about the overall purpose for the writing works hand-in-hand with each trait. By establishing a clear purpose at the beginning, students will be able to focus on the goal: creating a strong piece of writing. When introducing the Strong Verb to students, have them think about the question, **What is the purpose of the writing?**

The Strong Verb directs you to the purpose of your writing which, in turn, helps you determine the appropriate ideas, organization, voice, word choice, sentence fluency, and conventions for your writing. If, for example, the Strong Verb lets you know that your purpose is to persuade, then your writing should contain thoughtful arguments that will convince your reader of your point. Ask yourself, "What purpose for writing does the strong verb convey?" "What words can I use to help make my purpose clear?" "What voice will best suit my purpose?" "How can I construct my sentences to help bring my idea to life?" "What is the best organization to make this piece of writing really work well?" "Are there things I could do with conventions to make sure that this piece of writing fulfills its purpose?"

Writing to Prompts in the Trait-Based Classroom: Content Areas   Scholastic Teaching Resources

R.A.F.T.S. Prompts Help Students Become Proficient in the Writing Modes

It takes lots of practice for students to become proficient in the modes of writing: narrative, expository, persuasive, descriptive, and imaginative. You can provide practice by adding a writing mode to your prompts to help students understand whether they need to tell a story, to inform or explain, to construct an argument, to paint a picture with words, or to create a new way of seeing things. It's easy. All you need to do is add a writing mode to the Format, as we've done in the samples below:

Narrative

Role:	endangered flying squirrel
Audience:	construction company president
Format:	narrative letter
Topic:	the story of your family and its life in the forest
Strong Verb:	relate

Imagine you are an <u>endangered flying squirrel</u>. Write a <u>narrative letter</u> to a <u>construction</u>
                (Role)   **(Format)**   **(Audience)**
<u>company president</u>, <u>relating</u> the <u>story of your family and its life in the forest</u> in hopes
           (Strong verb)   **(Topic)**
that it will change his mind about building a shopping center on the site.

Expository

Role:	journalist
Audience:	readers of an animal magazine
Format:	expository research notes
Topic:	why they are an important species to have in the world and what their contribution is to sustaining the environment
Strong Verb:	detail

You are a <u>journalist</u> responsible for gathering background information for an article
      (Role)
for the <u>readers</u> of a magazine called *Animals and Their Homes: Saving Habitats for*
   (Audience)
Endangered Species. Create <u>expository research notes</u> that <u>detail</u> <u>why they are an</u>
                            (Format)   **(Strong verb)**
<u>important species to have in the world and what their contribution is to sustaining</u>
                              (Topic)
<u>the environment</u>.

PERSUASIVE

Role:	head of your town's endangered animals committee
Audience:	shopping center owner
Format:	persuasive e-mail
Topic:	choose another location for the shopping center in order to avoid displacing the endangered flying squirrel population
Strong Verb:	convince

You are the <u>head of your town's endangered animals committee</u> and have just found
      (Role)
out that a construction company is clearing a forest to build a shopping center. Write

a <u>persuasive e-mail</u> to <u>convince</u> the <u>shopping center owner</u> to <u>choose another</u>
  (Format)   **(Strong verb)**   **(Audience)**
<u>location in order to avoid displacing the flying squirrel population</u>. Be sure to include
      (Topic)
at least three good arguments for your cause.

DESCRIPTIVE

Role:	endangered flying squirrel
Audience:	tourists
Format:	descriptive travel brochure
Topic:	the beauty of your forest and its value to hikers, campers, and nature lovers
Strong Verb:	enlighten

You are an <u>endangered flying squirrel</u> in the lush Southwest Forest. Create a <u>descriptive</u>
     (Role)   **(Format)**
<u>travel brochure</u> to <u>enlighten</u> <u>tourists</u> about <u>the beauty of your forest and its value to</u>
        (Strong verb) (Audience)   **(Topic)**
<u>hikers, campers, and nature lovers</u>. Use lots of details to create a picture in the reader's

mind of how lovely and serene your forest is, so that they will plan a visit.

IMAGINATIVE

Role:	endangered flying squirrel
Audience:	your children
Format:	imaginative bedtime story
Topic:	the story of how the flying squirrels first came to live in the Southwest Forest
Strong Verb:	tell

You are the father of an <u>endangered flying squirrel</u>. Write an <u>imaginative bedtime</u>
                     (Role)   **(Format)**
<u>story</u> to <u>tell</u> <u>your children</u>, built around <u>the story of how the flying squirrels first came</u>
(Strong verb) (Audience)   **(Topic)**
<u>to live in the Southwest Forest</u>. Include details that show how special the forest is to

flying squirrels and other animals who live there.

Ready-to-Use R.A.F.T.S. Prompts

The R.A.F.T.S. prompts on the following pages are organized into three sections: Math, Social Studies, and Science. Each section provides the standards, thematic strands, or traits upon which the prompts are based; filled-in R.A.F.T.S. grids; R.A.F.T.S. prompts in paragraph form; and references to reproducible prompts to photocopy and distribute to students. You can use the R.A.F.T.S. prompts as written or adapt them to meet your students' needs.

Choose a R.A.F.T.S. prompt and write it on the board or overhead projector, or make copies of the reproducible version (pages 65–77) and give one to each student. Review the prompt with students, encourage them to think about each component carefully, and have them organize their ideas using the Thinking Sheet on pages 15–16. From there, have them draft, revise, edit, and publish their pieces.

You can adapt these R.A.F.T.S. prompts or create new ones by brainstorming your own components. Just make copies of the blank R.A.F.T.S. grid on page 79 and fill them in.

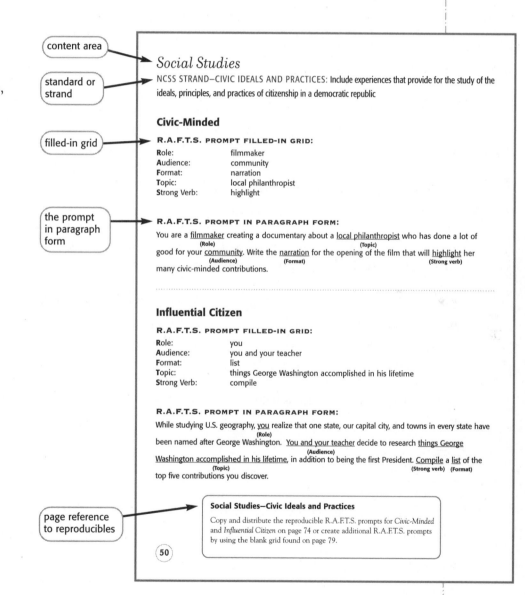

content area

standard or strand

filled-in grid

the prompt in paragraph form

page reference to reproducibles

Social Studies

NCSS STRAND—CIVIC IDEALS AND PRACTICES: Include experiences that provide for the study of the ideals, principles, and practices of citizenship in a democratic republic

Civic-Minded

R.A.F.T.S. PROMPT FILLED-IN GRID:

Role: filmmaker
Audience: community
Format: narration
Topic: local philanthropist
Strong Verb: highlight

R.A.F.T.S. PROMPT IN PARAGRAPH FORM:

You are a filmmaker creating a documentary about a local philanthropist who has done a lot of
         (Role)   (Topic)
good for your community. Write the narration for the opening of the film that will highlight her
         (Audience)   (Format)   (Strong verb)
many civic-minded contributions.

Influential Citizen

R.A.F.T.S. PROMPT FILLED-IN GRID:

Role: you
Audience: you and your teacher
Format: list
Topic: things George Washington accomplished in his lifetime
Strong Verb: compile

R.A.F.T.S. PROMPT IN PARAGRAPH FORM:

While studying U.S. geography, you realize that one state, our capital city, and towns in every state have
                             (Role)
been named after George Washington. You and your teacher decide to research things George
                                          (Audience)   (Topic)
Washington accomplished in his lifetime, in addition to being the first President. Compile a list of the
         (Topic)   (Strong verb) (Format)
top five contributions you discover.

> **Social Studies—Civic Ideals and Practices**
>
> Copy and distribute the reproducible R.A.F.T.S. prompts for *Civic-Minded* and *Influential Citizen* on page 74 or create additional R.A.F.T.S. prompts by using the blank grid found on page 79.

50

PREWRITING THINKING FOR R.A.F.T.S. PROMPTS

Once you've introduced students to the basic idea behind R.A.F.T.S. and have given them a prompt, it's time to get them thinking about what they will write. You can do this by introducing the following questions, which will help them make connections between the R.A.F.T.S. components and the information they will need to complete their writing.

1   To understand their role in writing the piece, have students ask themselves what they know about this role. How does this person speak? What special vocabulary or language might he or she use?

2   To understand their audience, have students ask themselves what they know about the reader for whom the piece is intended. What information does this audience need to know? What is an appropriate voice? What is the reaction students want from the audience?

3   Have students ask themselves the best way to organize their ideas to support the format specified in the prompt. Should they present information chronologically? Should they compare and/or contrast it? Should they use deductive logic? Should they develop a central theme?

4   To address their topic well, have students ask themselves what sorts of details to include to grab the audiences' attention. What do students already know about the topic? What questions should they answer for the reader?

5   To understand the purpose of the piece, have students think about the strong verb. What does the strong verb suggest they do? Persuade their audience? Explain something? Describe something? Tell a story? Use their imagination?

The reproducible R.A.F.T.S. Thinking Sheet on the next two pages can help your students make these connections before they start writing. Just photocopy as many as you need.

R.A.F.T.S. Thinking Sheet

Name: _____ **Date:**_____

HOW TO USE THIS SHEET:

When you are given a R.A.F.T.S. prompt, it's important to think about each component before you start writing. For example, look at this prompt:

You are the <u>writer of a children's book</u> that you want to get published. Write a
          (Role)

<u>cover letter</u> to the <u>editor</u> at the publishing house that <u>explains</u> <u>what your book is</u>
  (Format)   **(Audience)**   **(Strong verb)**

<u>about, why she should publish it, and why you are qualified to be an author.</u>
                    (Topic)

Then ask yourself these questions about each component:

Role: What do I know about writers of children's books?

Audience: What information would an editor need in order to make a decision about publishing my manuscript? What sort of voice should I use to convince her?

Format: What does a cover letter look like? How is it organized?

Topic: What sorts of things should be included in the letter in order to get the editor's attention?

Strong Verb: Since I am going to "explain" something to the editor, my purpose is to inform. As a writer, how do I accomplish that?

Now, by filling out this sheet, apply this thinking to the R.A.F.T.S. prompt that your teacher has given you.

(1) ROLE
What do I know about this role?_____

_____

What special language might a person in this role use? _____

_____

(2) AUDIENCE
What do I know about this audience? _____

_____

Writing to Prompts in the Trait-Based Classroom: Content Areas   *Scholastic Teaching Resources*

What information does this audience need to know? _____

_____

What voice would be most appropriate for this audience? _____

_____

(3) FORMAT

What do I know about this format? _____

_____

How are ideas typically organized for this format?

compare/contrast   cause and effect   point-by-point analysis

chronological order   deductive logic   development of a central theme

                                                            other:_____

(4) TOPIC

What do I know about this topic? _____

_____

What details should I provide for my audience? _____

_____

What questions should I answer for my audience? _____

_____

Where can I go to find more information if I need it?

encyclopedias   Internet   reference materials

periodicals   an expert in the field   other:_____

newspapers   library

(5) STRONG VERB

What purpose for my writing does this verb suggest? To inform or explain? To persuade?
To describe? To tell a story? To create a new way of seeing things? Some other purpose?

_____

What key words will make my purpose clear? _____

_____

Writing to Prompts in the Trait-Based Classroom: Content Areas Scholastic Teaching Resources

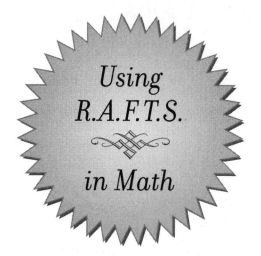

Using R.A.F.T.S. in Math

Who needs to write in math? Everyone! That's the consensus these days if we want students to understand math, apply it to solve problems, and use it in everyday life. This group of R.A.F.T.S. prompts has been designed to help you help students do exactly that. Organized around National Council of Teachers of Mathematics (NCTM) standards, these prompts invite students to apply the language and concepts of math in their writing. As a result, students become familiar with math terms and develop skills in the following areas:

- Number and Operations
- Algebra
- Geometry
- Measurement
- Data Analysis and Probability

- Problem Solving
- Reasoning and Proof
- Communication
- Connections
- Representation

Not all the R.A.F.T.S. prompts in this section contain the numbers necessary to do computations. For some, students will need to come up with their own numbers, based on what they know or what they learn from research about the topic; or, you can provide them with the numbers they need. As always, you can adapt the role, audience, format, topic, and strong verb of the R.A.F.T.S. to suit your instructional needs. These prompts are a place to begin the important work of writing about math.

The NCTM standard upon which each prompt is based appears above the fill-in grid. Of course, there are thousands of ways to address each standard, but we offer one as an example. You can create your own math R.A.F.T.S. prompts by referring to the Creating Your Own R.A.F.T.S. Prompts section on pages 78–80 and by using the reproducible blank grid on page 79.

Math—Number and Operations

Restaurant Dilemma

NCTM STANDARD: Understand numbers, ways of representing numbers, relationships among numbers, and number systems

R.A.F.T.S. PROMPT FILLED-IN GRID:

Role:	you
Audience:	restaurant manager
Format:	comment card
Topic:	an accurate total for your dinner bill
Strong Verbs:	revise and express

R.A.F.T.S. PROMPT IN PARAGRAPH FORM:

You are eating out with your family at a local restaurant. You order three hamburgers with French fries at $6.59 each, one chicken salad at $8.49, two iced teas at $1.39 each, three sodas at $1.39 each, and six desserts at $3.99 each. But when you receive your bill, you realize you've been charged for an extra soda and two extra desserts. Revise your bill to get an accurate total. Then
(Strong verb)   (Topic)

write a comment card to the manager, expressing your concern that you have been overcharged
    (Format)   (Audience) (Strong verb)   (Role)

and show how you corrected the error.

. . . .

Field Trip Preparation

NCTM STANDARD: Understand meanings of operations and how they relate to one another

R.A.F.T.S. PROMPT FILLED-IN GRID:

Role:	supervisor of transportation
Audience:	teacher
Format:	e-mail
Topic:	how much it will cost to take a field trip
Strong Verb:	explain

R.A.F.T.S. PROMPT IN PARAGRAPH FORM:

You are the <u>supervisor of transportation</u> for a local school district. Write an <u>e-mail</u> to a <u>teacher</u> who
          (Role)   **(Format)**   **(Audience)**
needs to know <u>how much it will cost to take a field trip</u> to the art museum, which is 20 miles away.
                                    (Topic)
In your message, <u>explain</u> the cost of transportation, knowing that the bus you plan to use gets nine
                    (Strong verb)
miles per gallon of gasoline, and the going rate for gasoline these days is $1.59 per gallon.

Math Problem for All

NCTM STANDARD: Compute fluently and make reasonable estimates

R.A.F.T.S. PROMPT FILLED-IN GRID:

Role:	top math student
Audience:	your classmates
Format:	overhead transparency
Topic:	the problem 56 x 22
Strong Verb:	create

R.A.F.T.S. PROMPT IN PARAGRAPH FORM:

You are a <u>top math student</u> and your teacher has asked you to help <u>your classmates</u> with a
            (Role)   **(Audience)**
math problem. <u>Create</u> an <u>overhead transparency</u> to demonstrate how you would solve
            (Strong verb)   **(Format)**
<u>the problem 56 x 22</u>. Be sure you include each step in your process so that your classmates will
      (Topic)
understand how you came up with the correct answer.

Math—Number and Operations

Copy and distribute the reproducible R.A.F.T.S. prompts for *Restaurant Dilemma, Field Trip Preparation,* and *Math Problem for All* on page 65 or create additional R.A.F.T.S. prompts by using the blank grid found on page 79.

Real-Life Algebra

NCTM STANDARD: Understand patterns, relations, and functions

R.A.F.T.S. PROMPT FILLED-IN GRID:

Role: you
Audience: your teacher
Format: journal entry
Topic: algebra solves everyday math problems
Strong Verb: contemplate

R.A.F.T.S. PROMPT IN PARAGRAPH FORM:

<u>Your teacher</u> has introduced your class to algebra and has stressed how useful it will be in life. Write
   (Audience)

a <u>journal entry</u> <u>contemplating</u> how <u>algebra will help you solve everyday math problems</u> and
  (Format)   (Strong verb)   (Topic)

whether <u>you</u> are sold on the idea or think it is just going to make things more confusing.
    (Role)

"Believe It or Not" Algebra Formula

NCTM STANDARD: Represent and analyze mathematical situations and structures using algebraic symbols

R.A.F.T.S. PROMPT FILLED-IN GRID:

Role: math student
Audience: you
Format: "Believe It or Not" journal
Topic: longest algebraic formula
Strong Verb: explain

R.A.F.T.S. PROMPT IN PARAGRAPH FORM:

<u>You</u> are a <u>math student</u> who keeps a <u>"Believe It or Not" journal</u> filled with fascinating mathematical
(Audience)   (Role)   (Format)

information. The latest entry is the <u>longest algebraic formula</u> that can be solved. Write about this
         (Topic)

discovery, <u>explain</u> where you found it and describe how it was originally used.
   (Strong verb)

Game Night

NCTM STANDARD: Use mathematical models to represent and understand quantitative relationships

R.A.F.T.S. PROMPT FILLED-IN GRID:

Role:	parent
Audience:	school principal
Format:	letter
Topic:	how many people can attend game night
Strong Verb:	calculate

R.A.F.T.S. PROMPT IN PARAGRAPH FORM:

You are a <u>parent</u> planning a school "game night" and have obtained from the city fire chief the
     (Role)
formula for determining maximum room capacity. Apply the formula he provided to the dimensions

of the gym to <u>calculate</u> <u>how many people can attend game night</u>. Then write a <u>letter</u> to the <u>school</u>
     (Strong verb)   **(Topic)**   **(Format)**   **(Audience)**
<u>principal</u> including this information, so he'll approve your request to use the gym for this function.

Payday Payoff

NCTM STANDARD: Analyze change in various contexts

R.A.F.T.S. PROMPT FILLED-IN GRID:

Role:	payroll clerk
Audience:	employees
Format:	memo
Topic:	increase they can expect in their paychecks
Strong Verb:	explain

R.A.F.T.S. PROMPT IN PARAGRAPH FORM:

You are the <u>payroll clerk</u> for the local department store. Your supervisor has just approved a five
     (Role)
percent cost-of-living raise for all employees, effective immediately. Write a <u>memo</u> to <u>employees</u>
                                                     (Format)   **(Audience)**
<u>explaining</u> how much of an <u>increase they can expect in their paychecks in terms of dollars</u>.
(Strong verb)   **(Topic)**

> ### Math—Algebra
>
> Copy and distribute the reproducible R.A.F.T.S. prompts for *Real-Life Algebra*, *"Believe It or Not" Algebra Formula*, *Game Night*, and *Payday Payoff* on pages 65–66 or create additional R.A.F.T.S. prompts by using the blank grid found on page 79.

Math—Geometry

Geometric Homes

NCTM STANDARD: Analyze the characteristics and properties of two- and three-dimensional geometric shapes and develop mathematical arguments about geometric relationships

R.A.F.T.S. PROMPT FILLED-IN GRID:

Role: head architect
Audience: president of Geometric Homes
Format: advertisement
Topic: four new homes
Strong Verb: design

R.A.F.T.S. PROMPT IN PARAGRAPH FORM:

Geometric Homes, a cutting-edge architecture firm, bases all of its designs on geometric shapes. As its <u>head architect</u>, you are asked to <u>design</u> an <u>advertisement</u> for the <u>president of Geometric Homes</u>
        (Role)   (Strong verb)   (Format)   (Audience)
to review, showcasing <u>four new homes</u>. In your advertisement, include appropriate names and
                            (Topic)
descriptions for each one.

Backyard Grids

NCTM STANDARD: Specify locations and describe spatial relationships using coordinate geometry and other representational systems

R.A.F.T.S. PROMPT FILLED-IN GRID:

Role: you
Audience: your dad
Format: grid
Topic: location of holes in backyard
Strong Verb: point out

R.A.F.T.S. PROMPT IN PARAGRAPH FORM:

Your dog has dug holes in the backyard and your dad is afraid he will step in them as he mows the lawn. <u>You</u> think you know how you can help. Create a <u>grid</u> of the backyard for <u>your dad</u>,
        (Role)   (Format)   (Audience)
<u>pointing out</u> the exact <u>location of each of the holes</u> in order to avoid mishaps.
(Strong verb)   (Topic)

Baseball Field

NCTM STANDARD: Apply transformations and use symmetry to analyze mathematical situations

R.A.F.T.S. PROMPT FILLED-IN GRID:

Role: student group
Audience: local school committee
Formats: cover letter and design plan
Topic: approval of the plan
Strong Verb: create

R.A.F.T.S. PROMPT IN PARAGRAPH FORM:

As part of a <u>student group</u> in your math class, you are working on plans for a new baseball
         (Role)
field. <u>Create</u> a final <u>design plan</u> and <u>cover letter</u> to submit to the <u>local school committee</u> for
  (Strong verb)   **(Format)**   **(Format)**   **(Audience)**
<u>approval of the plan</u>, to make sure it meets regulations.
  (Topic)

Puzzle Design

NCTM STANDARD: Use visualization, spatial reasoning, and geometric modeling to solve problems

R.A.F.T.S. PROMPT FILLED-IN GRID:

Role: toy designer
Audience: kids
Formats: puzzle and simple instructions
Topic: puzzles in geometric shapes
Strong Verbs: design and include

R.A.F.T.S. PROMPT IN PARAGRAPH FORM:

You are a <u>toy designer</u> who works in the puzzle department of Ricardo's Toy Company. The sales
    (Role)
team has reported to you that <u>kids</u> really like colorful <u>puzzles in geometric shapes</u>. <u>Design</u> a
          (Audience)   **(Topic)**   **(Strong verb)**
<u>puzzle</u> with this in mind, fashioning it so that all the pieces interlock. Give your puzzle a catchy
(Format)
name and <u>include</u> a few <u>simple instructions</u> on how to assemble it.
      (Strong verb)   **(Format)**

> **Math—Geometry**
>
> Copy and distribute the reproducible R.A.F.T.S. prompts for *Geometric Homes*,
> *Backyard Grids*, *Baseball Field*, and *Puzzle Design* on page 66 or create additional
> R.A.F.T.S. prompts by using the blank grid found on page 79.

Math—Measurement

Kilometers to Miles

NCTM STANDARD: Understand measurable attributes of objects and the units, systems, and processes of measurement

R.A.F.T.S. PROMPT FILLED-IN GRID:

Role: you
Audience: your family
Format: step-by-step instructions
Topic: converting kilometers to miles
Strong Verb: generate

R.A.F.T.S. PROMPT IN PARAGRAPH FORM:

Your father just bought a new European car with an odometer that shows distance in kilometers, not miles. Since this might take getting used to for <u>you</u>, your parents, and siblings, <u>generate</u>
                                                 (Role)   **(Strong verb)**
<u>step-by-step instructions</u> that <u>your family</u> can use for <u>converting kilometers to miles</u>.
     (Format)   **(Audience)**   **(Topic)**

Substitute Schedules

NCTM STANDARD: Apply appropriate techniques, tools, and formulas to determine measurements

R.A.F.T.S. PROMPT FILLED-IN GRID:

Role: you and your classmates
Audience: the substitute
Format: schedules in fifteen-minute time periods
Topic: an everyday schedule and a dream-day schedule
Strong Verb: create

R.A.F.T.S. PROMPT IN PARAGRAPH FORM:

Your teacher is taking a day off to attend a conference and has asked the class to <u>create</u> a daily
                                                          (Strong verb)
schedule for <u>the substitute</u>. <u>You and your classmates</u> decide to write <u>two schedules broken down</u>
              (Audience)   **(Role)**   **(Format)**
<u>into fifteen-minute time periods</u>: <u>1) the typical everyday schedule and 2) the schedule of your</u>
                                         (Topic)
<u>dream day at school</u>.

Math—Measurement

Copy and distribute the reproducible R.A.F.T.S. prompts for *Kilometers to Miles* and *Substitute Schedules* on pages 66–67 or create additional R.A.F.T.S. prompts by using the blank grid found on page 79.

Math—Data Analysis and Probability

Lunch Menus

NCTM STANDARD: Formulate questions that can be addressed with data and collect, organize, and display relevant data to answer them

R.A.F.T.S. PROMPT FILLED-IN GRID:

Role: spokesperson
Audience: school lunch officials
Format: letter
Topic: new meals
Strong Verb: argue

R.A.F.T.S. PROMPT IN PARAGRAPH FORM:

Your classmates are interested in changing the school lunch menus and have selected you as their

<u>spokesperson</u>. After surveying the student body to collect information about healthy yet tasty meals,
   (Role)

write a <u>letter</u> to <u>the school lunch officials</u>, <u>arguing</u> for <u>new meals</u> students would enjoy. Include the data
  (Format)   **(Audience)**   **(Strong verb)**   **(Topic)**
you collected in your letter to help build your case.

Perennial Growth

NCTM STANDARD: Select and use appropriate statistical methods to analyze data

R.A.F.T.S. PROMPT FILLED-IN GRID:

Role: lab assistant
Audience: your boss
Format: final report
Topic: growth cycle of perennial flowers
Strong Verb: prepare

R.A.F.T.S. PROMPT IN PARAGRAPH FORM:

You are a botanist's <u>lab assistant</u>. For the past few weeks, you have been collecting data on the
                          (Role)

<u>growth cycle of perennial flowers</u> during their first three years of life. Now you are ready to share
        (Topic)

your findings with <u>your boss</u>. <u>Prepare</u> a <u>final report</u> with charts, tables, or graphs that best display
               (Audience) **(Strong verb)**   **(Format)**

the information you have collected.

- -

Baseball Fame

NCTM STANDARD: Develop and evaluate inferences and predictions that are based on data

R.A.F.T.S. PROMPT FILLED-IN GRID:

Role:	high school baseball player
Audience:	sports card company executive
Format:	e-mail
Topic:	player statistics
Strong Verb:	predict

R.A.F.T.S. PROMPT IN PARAGRAPH FORM:

You are a <u>high school baseball player</u>. A <u>sports card company executive</u> is interested in putting your
              (Role)   **(Audience)**

photo and statistics on a baseball card as part of a series focusing on young players. At the

executive's request, <u>predict</u> your <u>home runs, batting average, and runs batted in for the forthcoming</u>
              (Strong verb)   **(Topic)**

<u>year</u> based on your performance from past seasons, and send the information to him in an <u>e-mail</u>.
                                                             (Format)

- -

Friday Night at the Movies

NCTM STANDARD: Understand and apply basic concepts of probability

R.A.F.T.S. PROMPT FILLED-IN GRID:

Role:	you
Audience:	one of your friends
Format:	script of a phone conversation
Topic:	probability of your parents letting you go to the movies
Strong Verb:	create

R.A.F.T.S. PROMPT IN PARAGRAPH FORM:

One of your favorite things to do is go to the movies with your friends on Friday nights. However,

this week one of your teachers called to inform your parents that you haven't been doing your

homework. <u>Create</u> the <u>script of a phone conversation</u> between <u>you</u> and <u>one of your friends,</u>
         (Strong verb)   **(Format)**   **(Role)**   **(Audience)**

discussing the <u>probability of your parents letting you go to the movies</u> this week.
              (Topic)

> ### Math—Data Analysis and Probability
>
> Copy and distribute the reproducible R.A.F.T.S. prompts for *Lunch Menus*, *Perennial Growth*, *Baseball Fame*, and *Friday Night at the Movies* on page 67 or create additional R.A.F.T.S. prompts by using the blank grid found on page 79.

Math—Problem Solving

Math Game

NCTM STANDARD: Build new mathematical knowledge through problem solving

R.A.F.T.S. PROMPT FILLED-IN GRID:

Role: you
Audience: one of your friends
Format: ten game cards
Topic: everyday math problem
Strong Verb: create

R.A.F.T.S. PROMPT IN PARAGRAPH FORM:

<u>One of your friends</u> is having a hard time understanding math operations. So it's up to <u>you</u> to <u>create</u>
   (Audience)   **(Role) (Strong verb)**

<u>ten game cards,</u> each with an <u>everyday math problem</u>. On the back of each card, record the best
   (Format)   **(Topic)**

operation to solve the problem. For example, if the problem for the front of the card reads, "If I received

23 e-mails each day for a week, how many e-mails do I get by the end of the week?" the answer on

the back should be "multiplication."

Recipe Remedy

NCTM STANDARD: Solve problems that arise in mathematics and in other contexts

R.A.F.T.S. PROMPT FILLED-IN GRID:

Role: pie-loving son or daughter
Audience: you and your mom
Format: new recipe
Topic: take the original recipe and triple it
Strong Verb: record

R.A.F.T.S. PROMPT IN PARAGRAPH FORM:

Your mother has agreed to help you bake your favorite pie. As a <u>pie-loving son or daughter,</u> <u>take the</u>
                                                                        (Role)
<u>original recipe for one pie and triple it</u> so that there is enough pie for everyone in the family. <u>Record</u> the
              (Topic)   (Strong verb)
<u>new recipe</u> so that <u>you and your mom</u> can start baking.
   (Format)   (Audience)

The Challenge of 10

NCTM STANDARD: Apply and adapt a variety of appropriate strategies to solve problems

R.A.F.T.S. PROMPT FILLED-IN GRID:

Role: you and your classmates
Audience: whole class
Formats: list and chart
Topic: problems with the answer "10"
Strong Verbs: compare and make

R.A.F.T.S. PROMPT IN PARAGRAPH FORM:

<u>You and a small group of classmates</u> have been given the challenge to come up with as many
                  (Role)
<u>problems</u> as possible <u>with the answer "10."</u> You can use fractions, decimals, number patterns—
   (Topic)
whatever makes sense. Once your group has created a <u>list</u> of problems, <u>compare</u> it with the other
                                                      (Format)   (Strong verb)
groups' lists and <u>make</u> a <u>chart</u> for the <u>whole class</u> of all the possibilities.
                  (Strong verb) (Format)   (Audience)

Doghouse

NCTM STANDARD: Monitor and reflect on the process of mathematical problem solving

R.A.F.T.S. PROMPT FILLED-IN GRID:

Role: you
Audience: you
Format: revised design
Topic: dimensions of the new doghouse
Strong Verb: create

R.A.F.T.S. PROMPT IN PARAGRAPH FORM:

<u>You</u> are building a new doghouse for your puppy. You have a design that will fit the puppy perfectly
(Role/Audience)
now. However, you realize that he will grow and, therefore, you need to accommodate his maximum

size. Estimate how large you think your puppy will become, figure out <u>the dimensions of the new</u>
(Topic)

<u>doghouse</u>, and <u>create</u> a <u>revised design</u>.
         (Strong verb)   **(Format)**

> **Math—Problem Solving**
>
> Copy and distribute the reproducible R.A.F.T.S. prompts for *Math Game,
> Recipe Remedy, The Challenge of 10,* and *Doghouse* on pages 67–68 or
> create additional R.A.F.T.S. prompts by using the blank grid found on
> page 79.

Math—Reasoning and Proof

Everyday Math

NCTM STANDARD: Recognize reasoning and proof as fundamental aspects of mathematics

R.A.F.T.S. PROMPT FILLED-IN GRID:

Role: math tutor
Audience: students
Format: story problem
Topic: multiplication used in everyday life
Strong Verbs: think and write

You are a <u>math tutor</u> at a local elementary school. You have been asked by the teachers to help
        (Role)

<u>students</u> understand the importance of mathematics by connecting math to real-life situations. <u>Think</u> of
(Audience)   (Strong verb)

two examples where <u>multiplication is used in everyday life</u> and <u>write</u> them out in a <u>story problem</u> for
                               (Topic)   (Strong verb)   (Format)

your students to solve in tutoring sessions.

Rows of Carrots

NCTM STANDARD: Make and investigate mathematical conjectures

R.A.F.T.S. PROMPT FILLED-IN GRID:

Role: vegetable gardener
Audience: yourself
Format: plan
Topic: rows of carrots
Strong Verbs: figure and write

R.A.F.T.S. PROMPT IN PARAGRAPH FORM:

You are a <u>vegetable gardener</u> who is planning your spring crop of carrots. You know that if you
           (Role/Audience)

plant one row, you will get enough carrots for several family meals, but you would like more than

that. <u>Figure</u> out <u>how many rows of carrots</u> you think you will need to keep your family fed for at
   (Strong verb)   (Topic)

least a month. <u>Write</u> out your <u>plan</u> so that you know how many seeds to plant.
      (Strong verb)   (Format)

Math Discussion

NCTM STANDARD: Develop and evaluate mathematical arguments and proofs

R.A.F.T.S. PROMPT FILLED-IN GRID:

Role: you
Audience: your best friend
Format: list
Topic: daily activities using math
Strong Verbs: share and specify

R.A.F.T.S. PROMPT IN PARAGRAPH FORM:

<u>You</u> and your best friend are having a heated discussion about math. Your friend says there's no
(Role)
room for math in everyday life. You disagree. To convince your friend, make a <u>list</u> of <u>activities that</u>
(Format)
<u>might occur during the day and in which math is needed,</u> such as grocery shopping or planning a
(Topic)
building project. <u>Share</u> your list with <u>your friend</u>. <u>Specify</u> the approach that is required to carry out
(Strong verb)   **(Audience)**   **(Strong verb)**
each activity: addition, division, algebra, geometry, and so on.

Aquarium Troubles

NCTM STANDARD: Select and use various types of reasoning and methods of proof

R.A.F.T.S. PROMPT FILLED-IN GRID:

Role: you
Audience: pet store owner
Formats: plan and letter
Topics: amount of water your aquarium holds and ask for refund
Strong Verbs: design and write

R.A.F.T.S. PROMPT IN PARAGRAPH FORM:

<u>You</u> just went to a pet store and bought a used 20-gallon aquarium. After you get home, you get
(Role)
a gut-wrenching feeling that the tank will not hold that much water. <u>Design</u> a <u>plan</u> to determine
(Strong verb) **(Format)**
<u>the amount of water your aquarium holds</u>. When it turns out that it really does hold less than
(Topic)
20 gallons, <u>write</u> a <u>letter</u> to the <u>pet store owner</u> explaining how you determined that fact and
(Strong verb) **(Format)**   **(Audience)**
<u>ask for a refund</u>.
(Topic)

> ### Math—Reasoning and Proof
>
> Copy and distribute the reproducible R.A.F.T.S. prompts for *Everyday Math*, *Rows of Carrots*, *Math Discussion*, and *Aquarium Troubles* on pages 68–69 or create additional R.A.F.T.S. prompts by using the blank grid found on page 79.

Math—Communication

Graphic Communication

NCTM STANDARD: Organize and consolidate their mathematical thinking through communication

R.A.F.T.S. PROMPT FILLED-IN GRID:

Role: you
Audience: the class
Format: notes for your speech
Topic: top ten most densely populated countries in the world
Strong Verb: explain

R.A.F.T.S. PROMPT IN PARAGRAPH FORM:

<u>You</u> are expected to speak to <u>the class</u> about your graph or chart showing the <u>top ten most densely</u>
(Role)   (Audience)
<u>populated countries in the world</u>. In your <u>notes for your speech</u>, <u>explain</u> why you chose a particular
     (Topic)   (Format)   (Strong verb)
chart or graph as the best way to represent your data and the useful information you can glean from it.

Art and Mathematics

NCTM STANDARD: Communicate their mathematical thinking coherently and clearly to peers, teachers, and others

R.A.F.T.S. PROMPT FILLED-IN GRID:

Role: artist
Audience: young artists
Format: step-by-step instructions
Topic: how to draw human portraits based on photographs
Strong Verb: give

R.A.F.T.S. PROMPT IN PARAGRAPH FORM:

You are an experienced <u>artist</u> who is working with <u>young artists</u>. Today's lesson focuses on <u>how to draw</u>
        (Role)   (Audience)
<u>human portraits based on photographs</u>. <u>Give</u> your protégés <u>step-by-step instructions</u> for measuring the
     (Topic)   (Strong verb)   (Format)
face in the photograph and determining the accurate proportions for enlarging it onto paper.

Math Mania

NCTM STANDARD: Analyze and evaluate the mathematical thinking and strategies of others

R.A.F.T.S. PROMPT FILLED-IN GRID:

Role: reporter
Audience: Math Mania readers
Format: list of questions
Topic: strategies she recommends for getting children interested in everyday math
Strong Verb: interview

R.A.F.T.S. PROMPT IN PARAGRAPH FORM:

You are a <u>reporter</u> for the magazine <u>*Math Mania*</u>. For your next story, you plan to <u>interview</u> your
      (Role)   **(Audience)**   **(Strong verb)**
son's math teacher about <u>strategies she recommends for getting children interested in everyday</u>
                    (Topic)
<u>math</u>, such as planning a garden, making change, or assembling a puzzle. Write the <u>list of questions</u>
                      (Format)
you plan to ask.

Book Titles

NCTM STANDARD: Use the language of mathematics to express mathematical ideas precisely

R.A.F.T.S. PROMPT FILLED-IN GRID:

Role: children's book author
Audience: your publisher
Format: titles with subtitles
Topic: math operations
Strong Verb: express

R.A.F.T.S. PROMPT IN PARAGRAPH FORM:

You are a <u>children's book author</u> and <u>your publisher</u> has asked you to start thinking about writing a set
       (Role)   **(Audience)**
of six books about <u>math operations</u>—addition, subtraction, multiplication, division, algebra, and
         (Topic)
geometry. Write possible <u>titles with subtitles</u> for each book in order to catch a child's eye and <u>express</u>
           (Format)   **(Strong verb)**
the operation precisely. For example, you might call the book on addition *The Sum of It All: Quirky Facts*

About Addition.

Math—Communication

Copy and distribute the reproducible R.A.F.T.S. prompts for *Graphic Communication, Art and Mathematics, Math Mania,* and *Book Titles* on page 69 or create additional R.A.F.T.S. prompts by using the blank grid found on page 79.

Math—Connections

Temperature Control

NCTM STANDARD: Recognize and use connections among mathematical ideas

R.A.F.T.S. PROMPT FILLED-IN GRID:

Role: meteorologist
Audience: viewers
Format: short introduction to weather report
Topic: daily temperatures
Strong Verb: chart

R.A.F.T.S. PROMPT IN PARAGRAPH FORM:

You are a TV <u>meteorologist</u>. Each month, your report features the average daily temperature for the
       (Role)
month. <u>Chart</u> the <u>daily temperatures</u> on a graph to share with <u>viewers,</u> then write a <u>short introduction</u>
  (Strong verb)   (Topic)   (Audience)   (Format)
for your report that includes the average temperature.

Average Scores for a Grade

NCTM STANDARD: Understand how mathematical ideas interconnect and build on one another to produce a coherent whole

R.A.F.T.S. PROMPT FILLED-IN GRID:

Role: you
Audience: your parents
Format: reflection
Topic: average your grades to arrive at a median score
Strong Verbs: share and write

R.A.F.T.S. PROMPT IN PARAGRAPH FORM:

<u>You</u> keep your weekly math grades in a notebook. This week your teacher asked you to <u>average</u>
(Role)
<u>your grades to arrive at a median score</u> to <u>share</u> with your parents at a parent/teacher conference.
          (Topic)   **(Strong verb)**
Do this calculation, then <u>write</u> a <u>reflection</u> to share with <u>your parents</u> on how well you are
               (Strong verb) **(Format)**   **(Audience)**
succeeding in math.

Math Autobiography

NCTM STANDARD: Recognize and apply mathematics in contexts outside of mathematics

R.A.F.T.S. PROMPT FILLED-IN GRID:

Role: you
Audience: your teacher
Format: mathematical autobiography
Topic: first time you remember using math to solve a problem outside of school
Strong Verb: document

R.A.F.T.S. PROMPT IN PARAGRAPH FORM:

<u>You</u> have been asked by <u>your teacher</u> to keep a <u>mathematical autobiography</u>. <u>Document</u> for yourself
(Role)   **(Audience)**   **(Format)**   **(Strong verb)**
the <u>first time you remember using math to solve a problem outside of school</u>. Perhaps you were
                  (Topic)
keeping score at a ball game or helping your parents figure out how much fabric to buy to cover a

favorite old chair. Think back to a time when you were glad you had math to solve a real-world

problem.

> **Math—Connections**
>
> Copy and distribute the reproducible R.A.F.T.S. prompts for *Temperature Control*, *Average Scores for a Grade*, and *Math Autobiography* on pages 69–70 or create additional R.A.F.T.S. prompts by using the blank grid found on page 79.

Math—Representation

Desert Island

NCTM STANDARD: Create and use representations to organize, record, and communicate mathematical ideas

R.A.F.T.S. PROMPT FILLED-IN GRID:

Role: you
Audience: your loved ones
Format: symbols
Topic: keeping track of the days of the week or the months of the year
Strong Verb: re-create

R.A.F.T.S. PROMPT IN PARAGRAPH FORM:

<u>You</u> were stranded on a deserted island. You had no calendar to <u>keep track of the days of the week</u>
(Role)   (Topic)
<u>or the months of the year</u>, so you used the sand and a stick to create <u>symbols</u>. Now that you have
                                                                                 (Format)
returned home, <u>re-create</u> those symbols on paper so that you can share with <u>loved ones</u> how
                (Strong verb)   (Audience)
inventive you were.

- -

Count Your Errors

NCTM STANDARD: Select, apply, and translate among mathematical representations to solve problems

R.A.F.T.S. PROMPT FILLED-IN GRID:

Role: you
Audience: your friend
Format: tally marks
Topic: problem points when giving a speech
Strong Verb: note

R.A.F.T.S. PROMPT IN PARAGRAPH FORM:

<u>You</u> are giving a two-minute speech entitled "Principal for a Day." During a practice run, you ask a
(Role)
friend to count the number of times you pause, use "umm," or utter other short, distracting sounds.

<u>Your friend</u> does this by making <u>tally marks</u> at <u>problem points</u> on a printed copy of the speech.
  (Audience)   (Format)   (Topic)
Reread your speech from this marked copy, <u>noting</u> the marks in the text and making efforts to
                                          (Strong verb)
improve your performance.

Paper-Folding Contest

NCTM STANDARD: Use representations to model and interpret physical, social, and mathematical
phenomena

R.A.F.T.S. PROMPT FILLED-IN GRID:

Role:	you
Audience:	your best friend
Format:	contest rules
Topic:	how many times a piece of paper can be folded
Strong Verb:	proceed

R.A.F.T.S. PROMPT IN PARAGRAPH FORM:

<u>You</u> and <u>your best friend</u> have entered into a contest to see <u>how many times a piece of paper can</u>
(Role)   (Audience)   (Topic)
<u>be folded</u>. You believe that a larger piece of paper can be folded more times than a smaller one.

Your friend says that it will be the same number of folds no matter what size the paper. Write down

the <u>rules for your contest</u> and then <u>proceed</u> to go through the steps to figure out who is correct.
       (Format)   (Strong verb)

> **Math—Representation**
>
> Copy and distribute the reproducible R.A.F.T.S. prompts for *Desert Island, Count Your Errors,* and *Paper-Folding Contest* on page 70 or create additional R.A.F.T.S. prompts by using the blank grid found on page 79.

Using R.A.F.T.S. in Social Studies

What do students in Argentina and students in the U.S. have in common? How has technology helped to create a global economy? Do the rights of individuals outweigh the rights of groups? Many questions that intrigue students come from social studies. By using R.A.F.T.S. prompts, you can encourage students to write on timely topics and, in the process, make connections, analyze beliefs, and study attitudes inside and outside of school. This group of R.A.F.T.S. prompts, which is designed to support the ten thematic strands from the National Council for the Social Studies (NCSS), encourage students to write on interesting and important topics that are meaningful to them—the first step in getting students excited about writing:

- Culture
- Time, Continuity, and Change
- People, Places, and Environments
- Individual Development and Identity
- Individuals, Groups, and Institutions

- Power, Authority, and Governance
- Civic Ideals and Practices
- Science, Technology, and Society
- Global Connections
- Production, Distribution, and Consumption

For some of the R.A.F.T.S. prompts, students will be able to draw upon their existing knowledge of social studies. Others may need to do some research or you may need to supply them with the information necessary to get started. Be sure to provide the time and resources students need to gather information.

The NCSS thematic strand upon which prompts are based appear as headers throughout this section. Of course, there are thousands of ways to address the issues in each strand, but we offer a couple for each as examples. You can create your own social studies prompts by referring to the Creating Your Own R.A.F.T.S. Prompts section on pages 78–80 and by using the blank grid on page 79. Weaving writing into social studies and other content areas generates new ways for students to show what they know and can do—and when they show us that, we can tell if they are meeting important content standards.

Social Studies

NCSS STRAND—CULTURE: Include experiences that provide for the study of culture and cultural diversity

Travel Plans

R.A.F.T.S. PROMPT FILLED-IN GRID:

Role: assistant to the president of the United States
Audience: the president
Format: report
Topic: your choice of the top candidate
Strong Verb: summarize

R.A.F.T.S. PROMPT IN PARAGRAPH FORM:

As the <u>assistant to the president of the United States</u>, you are responsible for reviewing all
          (Role)
nominees for the position of U.S. Ambassador to Mexico. Write the final <u>report</u> you give to <u>the</u>
                                              (Format)
<u>president</u> for <u>your choice of the top candidate</u>, <u>summarizing</u> the reasons you think this person will
(Audience)   **(Topic)**   **(Strong verb)**
do a good job based on his or her beliefs, knowledge, values, and understanding of Mexican culture

and traditions.

American Culture

R.A.F.T.S. PROMPT FILLED-IN GRID:

Role: journalist
Audience: editor
Formats: list and paragraph
Topic: five most important American cultural events of the 1980's
Strong Verb: explain

R.A.F.T.S. PROMPT IN PARAGRAPH FORM:

You are a <u>journalist</u> for a national magazine who has been assigned to write an article about the
        (Role)
<u>five most important American cultural events of the 1980's</u>. Make a <u>list</u> of these events and write a
                 (Topic)   **(Format)**
short <u>paragraph</u> <u>explaining</u> the importance of each one to submit to your <u>editor</u>.
     (Format)   **(Strong verb)**   **(Audience)**

Social Studies—Culture

Copy and distribute the reproducible R.A.F.T.S. prompts for *Travel Plans* and *American Culture* found on page 71 or create additional R.A.F.T.S. prompts by using the blank grid found on page 79.

Social Studies

NCSS STRAND—TIME, CONTINUITY, AND CHANGE: Include experiences that provide for the study of the ways human beings view themselves in and over time

Frontier Fantasy

R.A.F.T.S. PROMPT FILLED-IN GRID:

Role:	you
Audience:	producer for a local TV station
Format:	contest-entry essay
Topic:	knowledge of frontier life
Strong Verb:	impress

R.A.F.T.S. PROMPT IN PARAGRAPH FORM:

A <u>producer of a local TV station</u> is running a contest to choose a family to star in a new reality program
       (Audience)
about life in a frontier cabin for a month, in order to show what life was like in the nineteenth century.

<u>You</u> decide to write a <u>contest-entry essay</u> to <u>impress</u> the producer with your <u>knowledge of frontier life</u>.
(Role)   **(Format)**   **(Strong verb)**   **(Topic)**
Good luck!

Changes

R.A.F.T.S. PROMPT FILLED-IN GRID:

Role:	grandparent
Audience:	grandchildren
Format:	letter
Topic:	changes that have occurred over time in the way you shop
Strong Verb:	describe

R.A.F.T.S. PROMPT IN PARAGRAPH FORM:

You are a <u>grandparent</u> who was born in the 1930's. When you were young, you shopped at a
     (Role)
country store. As you got older, you shopped in supermarkets and department stores. Now you are

shopping on the Internet. Write a <u>letter</u> to your <u>grandchildren</u>, <u>describing</u> <u>the changes that have</u>
     (Format)   **(Audience)**   **(Strong verb)**   **(Topic)**
<u>taken place over time</u> in the way you buy things.

> **Social Studies—Time, Continuity, and Change**
>
> Copy and distribute the reproducible R.A.F.T.S. prompts for *Frontier Fantasy* and *Changes* on page 71 or create additional R.A.F.T.S. prompts by using the blank grid found on page 79.

Social Studies

NCSS STRAND—PEOPLE, PLACES, AND ENVIRONMENTS: Include experiences that provide
for the study of people, places, and environments

Places

R.A.F.T.S. PROMPT FILLED-IN GRID:

Role:	author of a new guidebook
Audience:	hikers
Format:	descriptions
Topic:	the top three hiking destinations
Strong Verbs:	suggest and recommend

R.A.F.T.S. PROMPT IN PARAGRAPH FORM:

You are the <u>author of a new guidebook</u> for <u>hikers</u> that <u>suggests</u> places to go hiking. Write
     (Role)   **(Audience)**   **(Strong verb)**
<u>descriptions</u> of the <u>top three destinations</u> that you highly <u>recommend</u>.
   (Format)   **(Topic)**   **(Strong verb)**

Environments

R.A.F.T.S. PROMPT FILLED-IN GRID:

Role: member of the science team for Biosphere 10
Audience: a family member
Format: e-mail
Topic: send a piece of clothing
Strong Verb: plead

R.A.F.T.S. PROMPT IN PARAGRAPH FORM:

You are a <u>member of the science team for Biosphere 10</u>. You will be living inside the biosphere for
(Role)

the next two years and have to wear only the clothes you packed and eat only the food you can

produce. You forgot one essential article of clothing, however. Write an <u>e-mail</u> to a <u>family member,</u>
(Format)   (Audience)

<u>pleading</u> with him or her to <u>send this important item</u> to you as soon as possible.
(Strong verb)   (Topic)

> ### Social Studies—People, Places, and Environments
>
> Copy and distribute the reproducible R.A.F.T.S. prompts for *Places* and *Environments* found on page 71 or create additional R.A.F.T.S. prompts by using the blank grid found on page 79.

Social Studies

NCSS STRAND—INDIVIDUAL DEVELOPMENT AND IDENTITY: Include experiences that provide for the study of individual development and identity

Identity Role

R.A.F.T.S. PROMPT FILLED-IN GRID:

Role: candidate for governor
Audience: TV audience
Format: interview script questions and answers
Topic: how you feel about an important campaign issue
Strong Verb: reveal

R.A.F.T.S. PROMPT IN PARAGRAPH FORM:

You are a <u>candidate for governor</u> of your state, and a correspondent from the local television station
     (Role)
is going to interview you. Write the <u>questions and answers</u> that will allow <u>viewers</u> to find <u>how you</u>
                              (Format)   **(Audience)**
<u>feel about an important campaign issue,</u> <u>reveal</u> who you are, and what you stand for.
          (Topic)   **(Strong verb)**

License Plate

R.A.F.T.S. PROMPT FILLED-IN GRID:

Role:	teenager
Audience:	other drivers
Format:	personalized license plate
Topic:	your distinct personality
Strong Verb:	convey

R.A.F.T.S. PROMPT IN PARAGRAPH FORM:

You are a <u>teenager</u> who has earned the money for your first car and you want to get <u>personalized</u>
       (Role)   **(Format)**
<u>license plates</u>. Design several possible license plate letter and number combinations that <u>convey</u>
                                                                              (Strong verb)
<u>your distinct personality</u> to <u>other drivers</u>.
        (Topic)   **(Audience)**

> ## Social Studies—Individual Development and Identity
>
> Copy and distribute the reproducible R.A.F.T.S. prompts for *Identity Role* and *License Plate* on page 72 or create additional R.A.F.T.S. prompts by using the blank grid found on page 79.

Social Studies

NCSS STRAND—INDIVIDUALS, GROUPS, AND INSTITUTIONS: Include experiences that provide for the study of interactions among individuals, groups, and institutions

Library Policy

R.A.F.T.S. PROMPT FILLED-IN GRID:

Role: you
Audience: other students
Format: poster
Topic: favorite book has been banned from the school library
Strong Verb: develop

R.A.F.T.S. PROMPT IN PARAGRAPH FORM:

As a student at your school, <u>you</u> just found out that your <u>favorite book has been banned from the</u>
                          (Role)   (Topic)
<u>school library</u>. You decide to call a meeting of <u>other students</u> who might be as concerned as you are
                                                              (Audience)
about this possibility. <u>Develop</u> the <u>poster</u> you will hang up in public areas, announcing the meeting.
                        (Strong verb)   (Format)

Dress Code

R.A.F.T.S. PROMPT FILLED-IN GRID:

Role: student representative
Audiences: student body, parents, teachers, and administrators
Format: questionnaire
Topic: change the school dress code to uniforms
Strong Verb: gather

R.A.F.T.S. PROMPT IN PARAGRAPH FORM:

You are the <u>student representative</u> for the local school committee. Some of the members would
                   (Role)
like to <u>change the school dress code to uniforms</u>. Write a <u>questionnaire</u> to be administered to
              (Topic)   (Format)
<u>the student body, parents, teachers, and administrators</u> to <u>gather</u> information about how each
              (Audience)   (Strong verb)
group feels about this proposed policy.

> ### Social Studies—Individuals, Groups, and Institutions
>
> Copy and distribute the reproducible R.A.F.T.S. prompts for *Library Policy* and *Dress Code* on page 72 or create additional R.A.F.T.S. prompts by using the blank grid found on page 79.

Social Studies

NCSS STRAND—POWER, AUTHORITY, AND GOVERNANCE: Include experiences that provide for the study of how people create and change structures of power, authority, and governance

Adopt-a-Park Campaign

R.A.F.T.S. PROMPT FILLED-IN GRID:

Role: student liaison
Audience: classmates
Format: campaign
Topic: a park near your school is going to be closing
Strong Verbs: appeal and design

R.A.F.T.S. PROMPT IN PARAGRAPH FORM:

You are the <u>student liaison</u> to the City Parks and Recreation Bureau. You find out that a <u>park near</u>
         (Role)
<u>your school is going to be closing</u> because it costs too much to maintain. However, if you can
    (Topic)
<u>appeal</u> to your fellow <u>classmates</u> to join the "Adopt-a-Park" program, there is a good chance the
(Strong verb)   **(Audience)**
park can stay open. <u>Design</u> the <u>campaign</u> to save your park, which consists of a poster, a bumper
      (Strong verb)   **(Format)**
sticker, and a lapel button.

Group Conflict Resolution

R.A.F.T.S. PROMPT FILLED-IN GRID:

Role: you
Audience: parents
Format: position paper
Topic: out-of-town tournament that takes place over Thanksgiving
Strong Verb: convince

R.A.F.T.S. PROMPT IN PARAGRAPH FORM:

Your soccer team has been invited to an <u>out-of-town tournament that takes place over</u>
          (Topic)
<u>Thanksgiving</u>. Some of the parents don't want their children to go, but <u>you</u> need everyone on the
      (Role)
team to be there if you stand any chance of winning. Develop a strongly worded <u>position paper</u> to
      (Format)
<u>convince</u> those <u>parents</u> to change their minds.
(Strong verb)   **(Audience)**

Social Studies—Power, Authority, and Governance

Copy and distribute the reproducible R.A.F.T.S. prompts for *Adopt-a-Park Campaign* and *Group Conflict Resolution* on page 72 or create additional R.A.F.T.S. prompts by using the blank grid found on page 79.

Social Studies

NCSS STRAND—PRODUCTION, DISTRIBUTION, AND CONSUMPTION: Include experiences that provide for the study of how people organize for the production, distribution, and consumption of goods and services

Public Notice

R.A.F.T.S. PROMPT FILLED-IN GRID:

Role: head of marketing
Audience: president of the company that distributes the game
Format: recall notice
Topic: virus in one of your computer games
Strong Verb: explain

R.A.F.T.S. PROMPT IN PARAGRAPH FORM:

You are the <u>head of marketing</u> for a company that manufactures computer games. You just found
(Role)
out there is a <u>virus in one of your games</u>. Write the <u>recall notice</u> you send to the <u>president of the</u>
(Topic)   (Format)   (Audience)
<u>company that distributes the game</u>, <u>explaining</u> the problem and how you plan to rectify it.
(Strong verb)

Book Demand

R.A.F.T.S. PROMPT FILLED-IN GRID:

Role: you
Audience: book publisher
Format: letter
Topic: not being able to get a copy of the new book
Strong Verb: express

R.A.F.T.S. PROMPT IN PARAGRAPH FORM:

The newest book in your favorite fantasy-fiction series is finally at the bookstore. When <u>you</u> get
(Role)
there, the manager tells you she is sold out and can't get more copies anytime soon. Write a <u>letter</u>
(Format)
to the <u>publisher</u> <u>expressing</u> your disappointment in <u>not being able to get a copy of the new book</u>.
(Audience) (Strong verb)   (Topic)
In your letter, suggest ways to avoid shortages in the future.

> **Social Studies—Production, Distribution, and Consumption**
>
> Copy and distribute the reproducible R.A.F.T.S. prompts for *Public Notice*
> and *Book Demand* found on page 73 or create additional R.A.F.T.S.
> prompts by using the blank grid found on page 79.

Social Studies

NCSS STRAND—SCIENCE, TECHNOLOGY, AND SOCIETY: Include experiences that provide for
the study of relationships among science, technology, and society

New Technology

R.A.F.T.S. PROMPT FILLED-IN GRID:

Role: technical writer
Audience: families
Format: easy-to-understand instructional manual
Topic: how to operate the robot
Strong Verb: inform

R.A.F.T.S. PROMPT IN PARAGRAPH FORM:

You are a <u>technical writer</u> who has been hired by an inventor to write an <u>easy-to-understand</u>
(Role)   (Format)
<u>instructional manual</u> for a new robot that every family will want because it can cook everyone's

favorite meals. Your manual should <u>inform</u> <u>families</u> of <u>how to operate the robot</u>.
(Strong verb) (Audience)   (Topic)

Space Debate

R.A.F.T.S. PROMPT FILLED-IN GRID:

Role: member of the NASA scientific panel
Audience: other panel members
Format: notes
Topic: whether Neil Armstrong actually landed on the moon or whether he was part of a technology hoax
Strong Verbs: present and support

R.A.F.T.S. PROMPT IN PARAGRAPH FORM:

Ever since the American public watched the televised moon landing in 1969, people have been

arguing about <u>whether Neil Armstrong actually landed on the moon or whether he was part of a</u>
                                                    (Topic)
<u>technology hoax</u>. NASA has put together a scientific research panel to put this issue to rest for once

and for all. As a <u>member of the panel</u>, write the <u>notes</u> that you will <u>present</u> to the <u>other members</u>
                         (Role)   **(Format)**   **(Strong verb)**   **(Audience)**
to <u>support</u> your position that the moon landing was real.
   (Strong verb)

Social Studies—Science, Technology, and Society

Copy and distribute the reproducible R.A.F.T.S. prompts for *New Technology* and *Space Debate* found on page 73 or create additional R.A.F.T.S. prompts by using the blank grid found on page 79.

Social Studies

NCSS STRAND—GLOBAL CONNECTIONS: Include experiences that provide for the study of global connections and interdependence

Human Rights

R.A.F.T.S. PROMPT FILLED-IN GRID:

Role: United States senator
Audience: citizens
Format: brief statement
Topic: new taxes being spent on building affordable housing
Strong Verb: propose

R.A.F.T.S. PROMPT IN PARAGRAPH FORM:

You are a <u>United States senator</u> who is concerned that housing is too costly for many of the <u>citizens</u>
        (Role)   **(Audience)**
of your state. Write the <u>brief statement</u> that comes at the beginning of a law you are <u>proposing</u> that
                       (Format)   **(Strong verb)**
calls for <u>new taxes being spent on building affordable housing</u>.
                       (Topic)

Environmental Greetings

R.A.F.T.S. PROMPT FILLED-IN GRID:

Role: you
Audience: parents and local community members
Format: text for scenic greeting cards
Topic: National Wildlife Week
Strong Verb: create

R.A.F.T.S. PROMPT IN PARAGRAPH FORM:

<u>You</u> and your classmates are creating <u>greeting cards</u> that you will sell during National Wildlife Week
(Role)   **(Format)**
to <u>raise money for the local animal shelter</u>. The cards feature photographs of local wildlife. <u>Create</u>
          (Topic)   **(Strong verb)**
the text for the cards that will appeal to <u>parents and other members of the community</u>.
                                                (Audience)

> ### Social Studies—Global Connections
>
> Copy and distribute the reproducible R.A.F.T.S. prompts for *Human Rights* and *Environmental Greetings* found on page 73 or create additional R.A.F.T.S. prompts by using the blank grid found on page 79.

Social Studies

NCSS STRAND—CIVIC IDEALS AND PRACTICES: Include experiences that provide for the study of the ideals, principles, and practices of citizenship in a democratic republic

Civic-Minded

R.A.F.T.S. PROMPT FILLED-IN GRID:

Role: filmmaker
Audience: community
Format: narration
Topic: local philanthropist
Strong Verb: highlight

R.A.F.T.S. PROMPT IN PARAGRAPH FORM:

You are a <u>filmmaker</u> creating a documentary about a <u>local philanthropist</u> who has done a lot of
        (Role)   (Topic)
good for your <u>community</u>. Write the <u>narration</u> for the opening of the film that will <u>highlight</u> her
          (Audience)   (Format)   (Strong verb)
many civic-minded contributions.

Influential Citizen

R.A.F.T.S. PROMPT FILLED-IN GRID:

Role: you
Audience: you and your teacher
Format: list
Topic: things George Washington accomplished in his lifetime
Strong Verb: compile

R.A.F.T.S. PROMPT IN PARAGRAPH FORM:

While studying U.S. geography, <u>you</u> realize that one state, our capital city, and towns in every state have
                                 (Role)
been named after George Washington. <u>You and your teacher</u> decide to research <u>things George</u>
                                     (Audience)
<u>Washington accomplished in his lifetime</u>, in addition to being the first President. <u>Compile</u> a <u>list</u> of the
                (Topic)   (Strong verb) (Format)
top five contributions you discover.

> ### Social Studies—Civic Ideals and Practices
>
> Copy and distribute the reproducible R.A.F.T.S. prompts for *Civic-Minded* and *Influential Citizen* on page 74 or create additional R.A.F.T.S. prompts by using the blank grid found on page 79.

Using R.A.F.T.S. in Science

The workings of systems, the intricacies of nature, the concepts of earth and space, and making sense of that information have fascinated students for generations. In science, the question "How come?" is a steady drumbeat toward students' understanding of the world around them. Writing is a powerful way to help apply students' scientific knowledge and communicate it to the world. The R.A.F.T.S. prompts in this section are designed to help students do just that by supporting the seven content-standard areas from the National Academy of Sciences (NAS):

- Science as Inquiry

- Physical Science

- Life Science

- Earth and Space Science

- Science and Technology

- Science in Personal and Social Perspectives

- History and Nature of Science

For some of the R.A.F.T.S. prompts, students will be able to draw upon their existing knowledge of science. But for others, they may need to do some research or you may need to supply them with the information necessary to get started. Be sure to provide the time and resources students need in order to gather information. Armed with the right information, students can use the R.A.F.T.S. prompt to create an interesting and informative piece that shows their scientific understanding.

The NAS content standard upon which each prompt is based appears above the fill-in grid. Of course, there are thousands of ways to address the issues in each standard, but we offer one as an example. You can create your own science prompts by referring to the Creating Your Own R.A.F.T.S. Prompts section on pages 78–80 and by using the blank grid on page 79. Thinking and writing like a scientist can go a long way toward helping students understand important science concepts and explain how things work in the world.

Science—Science as Inquiry

Scientific Inquiry in Action

NAS STANDARD: Develop abilities necessary to do scientific inquiry

R.A.F.T.S. PROMPT FILLED-IN GRID:

Role: marine life researcher
Audience: Web site visitors
Formats: a plan and list
Topic: poisonous fish found in the oceans of the world
Strong Verbs: compile and create

R.A.F.T.S. PROMPT IN PARAGRAPH FORM:

You are a <u>marine life researcher</u> and have been asked to <u>compile</u> information on <u>poisonous fish</u>
         (Role)   **(Strong verb)**
<u>found in the oceans of the world</u> for <u>visitors to your organization's Web site</u>. Write a <u>plan</u> describing
       (Topic)   **(Audience)**   **(Format)**
the steps you will take to find this information, carry out that plan, and <u>create</u> a <u>list</u> of the fish
                                       (Strong verb) (Format)
you locate.

Funding Scientific Research

NAS STANDARD: Develop understandings about scientific inquiry

R.A.F.T.S. PROMPT FILLED-IN GRID:

Role: research scientist
Audience: prospective donors
Format: fundraising letter
Topic: contribute money for equipment
Strong Verb: persuade

R.A.F.T.S. PROMPT IN PARAGRAPH FORM:

You are a <u>research scientist</u> who is working on an important project to discover cures for
        (Role)
communicable diseases. Your work requires special equipment that is very expensive. Write a

<u>fundraising letter</u> to send to <u>prospective donors,</u> <u>persuading</u> them to <u>contribute money for the</u>
   (Format)   **(Audience)**   **(Strong verb)**   **(Topic)**
<u>equipment</u>.

Science—Science as Inquiry

Copy and distribute the reproducible R.A.F.T.S. prompts for *Scientific Inquiry in Action* and *Funding Scientific Research* on page 74 or create additional R.A.F.T.S. prompts by using the blank grid found on page 79.

Science—Physical Science

Hardness of Minerals

NAS STANDARD: Develop an understanding of properties and changes of properties in matter

R.A.F.T.S. PROMPT FILLED-IN GRID:

Role:	you
Audience:	your classmates
Format:	poster with captions
Topic:	the hardness of five minerals and where they are commonly found
Strong Verb:	create

R.A.F.T.S. PROMPT IN PARAGRAPH FORM:

In science, <u>you</u> learn about common minerals and their uses. <u>Create</u> a <u>poster with captions</u> for your
      (Role)   **(Strong verb)**   **(Format)**

<u>classmates</u> that shows <u>the hardness of five minerals and where they are commonly found</u>.
   (Audience)   **(Topic)**

Motion and Forces in Racing

NAS STANDARD: Develop an understanding of motions and forces

R.A.F.T.S. PROMPT FILLED-IN GRID:

Role:	race car driver
Audience:	readers of *Racing Enthusiast's Monthly*
Format:	magazine article
Topic:	how your car's new, frictionless body style helped you win the race
Strong Verb:	express

R.A.F.T.S. PROMPT IN PARAGRAPH FORM:

As a <u>race car driver</u> who has just won your first race, write an <u>article</u> for <u>readers of *Racing</u>
    (Role)   (Format)   (Audience)
<u>Enthusiast's Monthly*</u> <u>expressing</u> how your <u>car's frictionless body style helped</u> lead you to victory.
                                    (Strong verb)   (Topic)
Be sure to thank your car designer and your sponsors for their support in making it all possible.

Energy that Keeps You Warm

NAS STANDARD: Develop an understanding of transfer of energy

R.A.F.T.S. PROMPT FILLED-IN GRID:

Role: tour director
Audience: students
Format: list
Topic: types of clothing for a winter tour
Strong Verb: create

R.A.F.T.S. PROMPT IN PARAGRAPH FORM:

You are the <u>tour director</u> for a group of <u>students</u> who are traveling through the United States over
            (Role)   (Audience)
winter break. <u>Create</u> a <u>list</u> of <u>types of clothing</u> they will need for stops in Florida, Maine, California,
            (Strong verb) (Format)   (Topic)
and Minnesota so that they will know exactly what to pack. Give examples of items of clothing you

recommend and explain why you recommend them.

> ### Science—Physical Science
>
> Copy and distribute the reproducible R.A.F.T.S. prompts for *Hardness of Minerals, Motions and Forces in Racing,* and *Energy that Keeps You Warm* on pages 74–75 or create additional R.A.F.T.S. prompts by using the blank grid found on page 79.

Science—Life Science

The Functions of Human Organs

NAS STANDARD: Develop understanding of structure and function in living systems

R.A.F.T.S. PROMPT FILLED-IN GRID:

Role: human brain
Audience: the other organs
Format: pep talk
Topic: keep digestion, respiration, and circulation in tip-top shape
Strong Verb: encourage

R.A.F.T.S. PROMPT IN PARAGRAPH FORM:

You are the <u>brain</u> in a human body and you notice that some organs are not working well to keep the
      (Role)
body functioning. Write a <u>pep talk</u> to give to <u>the organs</u>, <u>encouraging</u> them to <u>keep digestion,</u>
          (Format)   (Audience)   (Strong verb)
<u>respiration, and circulation in tip-top shape</u>. Be sure to include sound reasoning for your concerns.
     (Topic)

Learning About Heredity

NAS STANDARD: Develop understanding of reproduction and heredity

R.A.F.T.S. PROMPT FILLED-IN GRID:

Role: you
Audience: your family
Format: list with description
Topic: physical characteristics you inherited
Strong Verbs: make and describe

R.A.F.T.S. PROMPT IN PARAGRAPH FORM:

<u>You</u> have been looking through family albums and notice you have some <u>physical characteristics that</u>
(Role)   (Topic)
<u>you inherited from past generations</u>. Your height, hair color, the shape of your nose, and even your

build match those of relatives from both sides of your family. <u>Make</u> a <u>list</u> of these characteristics and
                                           (Strong verb)   (Format)
<u>describe</u> them in detail so that you can share the list with <u>family members</u> at an upcoming reunion.
(Strong verb)   (Audience)

Behavior and Care of Animals

NAS STANDARD: Develop understanding of regulation and behavior

R.A.F.T.S. PROMPT FILLED-IN GRID:

Role: pet store owner
Audience: new clerk
Format: set of instructions
Topic: how to keep an animal of your choice healthy and happy
Strong Verb: explain

R.A.F.T.S. PROMPT IN PARAGRAPH FORM:

You are a <u>pet store owner</u> and have just hired a new clerk to care for the animals while you're on
              (Role)
vacation. Write a <u>set of instructions</u> for the <u>clerk</u>, <u>explaining</u> <u>how to keep an animal of your choice</u>
              (Format)   (Audience) (Strong verb)   (Topic)
<u>healthy and happy</u>.

Ecosystem Skits

NAS STANDARD: Develop understanding of populations and ecosystems

R.A.F.T.S. PROMPT FILLED-IN GRID:

Role: the head of the local garden club
Audience: second-grade teacher and her students
Format: short skit
Topic: the roles of producers, consumers, and decomposers in a garden ecosystem
Strong Verb: demonstrate

R.A.F.T.S. PROMPT IN PARAGRAPH FORM:

You are the <u>head of the local garden club</u> and have been asked by a <u>second-grade teacher</u> to create
              (Role)   (Audience)
a fun way to help students learn about ecosystems. Write a <u>short skit</u> for <u>her students</u> to perform
                                    (Format)   (Audience)
that has parts for producers, consumers, and decomposers, and that <u>demonstrates</u> <u>how these roles</u>
                                                                    (Strong verb)   (Topic)
<u>work in an garden ecosystem</u>.

Discovery of New Life Form

NAS STANDARD: Develop understanding of diversity and adaptations of organisms

R.A.F.T.S. PROMPT FILLED-IN GRID:

Role: scuba diver
Audience: marine biologist at the local university
Format: letter
Topic: discovery of a new species of fish
Strong Verb: inquire

R.A.F.T.S. PROMPT IN PARAGRAPH FORM:

As an avid <u>scuba diver</u>, you think you might have <u>discovered a new species of fish</u> that lives in
          (Role)   **(Topic)**
shallow water. Write a <u>letter</u> to a <u>marine biologist</u> at the local university <u>inquiring</u> if she might be
            (Format)   **(Audience)**   **(Strong verb)**
interested in investigating your discovery. Include a detailed observation of how this new species

adapts to its environment, your detailed observations of the species, and what you'd like to name it.

> **Science—Life Science**
>
> Copy and distribute the reproducible R.A.F.T.S. prompts for *The Functions of Human Organs, Learning About Heredity, Behavior and Care of Animals, Ecosystem Skits,* and *Discovery of New Life Form* on page 75 or create additional R.A.F.T.S. prompts by using the blank grid found on page 79.

Science—Earth and Space Science

NAS STANDARD: Develop an understanding of structure of the earth system

The Water Cycle

R.A.F.T.S. PROMPT FILLED-IN GRID:

Role: single drop of ocean water
Audience: yourself
Format: trip log
Topic: the water cycle
Strong Verb: record

You are a single <u>drop of ocean water</u> that is beginning a trip through <u>the water cycle</u>. Write an
               (Role and Audience)   **(Topic)**
imaginative <u>trip log</u> to <u>record</u> your progress as you evaporate from the ocean, travel through the air,
         (Format)   **(Strong verb)**
rain down on the land, and flow back to the ocean.

Earthquake Alert

NAS STANDARD: Develop an understanding of Earth's history

R.A.F.T.S. PROMPT FILLED-IN GRID:

Role:	geologist
Audience:	people in earthquake-prone areas
Format:	TV commentary
Topic:	the dangers of earthquakes and their history in your region
Strong Verb:	alert

R.A.F.T.S. PROMPT IN PARAGRAPH FORM:

You are a <u>geologist</u> who studies the movement of the plates that make up the Earth's crust. Write a
        (Role)
<u>TV commentary</u> you might deliver to <u>people living on or near fault lines</u>, <u>alerting</u> them to <u>the</u>
  (Format)   **(Audience)**   **(Strong verb)**
<u>dangers of earthquakes and their history in your region.</u>
                     (Topic)

New Planet Discovery

NAS STANDARD: Develop an understanding of Earth in the solar system

R.A.F.T.S. PROMPT FILLED-IN GRID:

Role:	renowned astronomer
Audience:	leaders of the scientific community
Format:	announcement
Topic:	discovery of a new planet in orbit around the sun
Strong Verb:	proclaim

R.A.F.T.S. PROMPT IN PARAGRAPH FORM:

You are a <u>renowned astronomer</u> who has documented many comets and asteroids. Now, you have
       (Role)

discovered something even more exciting: <u>a new planet in orbit around the sun</u>. Write an
                                   (Topic)

<u>announcement</u> for the <u>leaders of the scientific community</u>, <u>proclaiming</u> your discovery. Include
 (Format)   **(Audience)**   **(Strong verb)**

specific details from your notes to authenticate your claim.

> ### Science— Life Science
>
> Copy and distribute the reproducible R.A.F.T.S. prompts for *The Water Cycle*, *Earthquake Alert*, and *New Planet Discovery* on pages 75–76 or create additional R.A.F.T.S. prompts by using the blank grid found on page 79.

Science—Science and Technology

Technology for Household Help

NAS STANDARD: Develop abilities of technological design

R.A.F.T.S. PROMPT FILLED-IN GRID:

Role:	you
Audience:	team of engineers
Format:	picture with captions
Topic:	machine that will clean your room
Strong Verb:	explain

R.A.F.T.S. PROMPT IN PARAGRAPH FORM:

<u>You</u> have entered a contest to design a <u>machine that will clean your room</u>. Draw a <u>picture</u> of your
(Role)   **(Topic)**   **(Format)**

machine with <u>captions</u> that <u>explain</u> how it works. If you win the contest, the <u>team of engineers</u> will
       (Format)   **(Strong verb)**   **(Audience)**

build your machine.

Designing for Market

NAS STANDARD: Develop understanding about science and technology

R.A.F.T.S. PROMPT FILLED-IN GRID:

Role: organic farmer
Audience: delivery company manager
Format: e-mail
Topic: a new container for tomatoes
Strong Verb: design

R.A.F.T.S. PROMPT IN PARAGRAPH FORM:

You are an <u>organic farmer</u> who has perfected a new way to grow more nutritious and delicious
         (Role)
tomatoes. In an <u>e-mail</u>, ask your <u>delivery company manager</u> to <u>design</u> a <u>new container that will get</u>
           (Format)   (Audience)   (Strong verb)   (Topic)
<u>your tomatoes to market without bruising</u>. Be sure to give all the information he needs to create a

proposal: the average size of the tomatoes, how far they will travel, and how long they need to stay

in the containers before they are sold.

> **Science—Science and Technology**
>
> Copy and distribute the reproducible R.A.F.T.S. prompts for *Technology for Household Help* and *Designing for Market* on page 76 or create additional R.A.F.T.S. prompts by using the blank grid found on page 79.

Science—Science in Personal and Social Perspectives

Exercise and Health

NAS STANDARD: Develop understanding of personal health

R.A.F.T.S. PROMPT FILLED-IN GRID:

Roles: an exercise guru and a couch potato
Audience: radio audience listeners
Format: debate
Topic: the pros and cons of daily exercise
Strong Verb: argue

Radio station KBY has scheduled a three-minute debate for <u>listeners</u> between an <u>exercise guru and</u>
                                                (Audience)   **(Role)**
<u>a couch potato</u>. Write the <u>debate</u> <u>arguing</u> the <u>pros and cons of daily exercise</u>. Include information
                (Format)   **(Strong verb)**   **(Topic)**
that grounds each argument in facts affecting health.

Maintaining Water Reserves

NAS STANDARD: Develop understanding of populations, resources, and environments

R.A.F.T.S. **PROMPT FILLED-IN GRID:**

Role:	concerned citizen
Audience:	city planner
Format:	letter
Topic:	water reservoir isn't large enough to supply all the new houses that are being built
Strong Verb:	alert

R.A.F.T.S. **PROMPT IN PARAGRAPH FORM:**

As a <u>concerned citizen</u>, write a <u>letter</u> to the <u>city planner</u> <u>alerting</u> him to the fact that the one and
           (Role)   **(Format)**   **(Audience)** **(Strong verb)**
only <u>water reservoir isn't large enough to supply all the new houses that are being built</u>. In your
                                    (Topic)
letter, include some alternative ways of supplying water to local homeowners and businesses.

Protecting Your Local Environment

NAS STANDARD: Develop understanding of natural hazards

R.A.F.T.S. **PROMPT FILLED-IN GRID:**

Role:	new resident
Audience:	neighbors and the committee
Format:	petition
Topic:	the environmental hazards of a landfill
Strong Verb:	create

R.A.F.T.S. PROMPT IN PARAGRAPH FORM:

You are a <u>new resident</u> in town and have just learned that the waste disposal committee is
       (Role)
planning to build a landfill near your house. <u>Create</u> a <u>petition</u> for your <u>neighbors</u> to sign that
       (Strong verb)   (Format)   (Audience)
informs them and <u>the committee</u> of <u>the environmental hazards of a landfill</u>, specifically that
       (Audience)   (Topic)
chemicals would leach into the local water supply.

- -

Marketing a New Car

NAS STANDARD: Develop understanding of risks and benefits

R.A.F.T.S. PROMPT FILLED-IN GRID:

Role: marketing executive of an automobile manufacturer
Audience: buyers
Format: brochure
Topic: benefits of this vehicle
Strong Verb: design

R.A.F.T.S. PROMPT IN PARAGRAPH FORM:

You are the <u>marketing executive of an automobile manufacturer</u> that is offering a revolutionary
       (Role)
new car that runs half on gas and half on electricity. <u>Design</u> a <u>brochure</u> informing <u>buyers</u> of the
       (Strong verb) (Format)   (Audience)
<u>benefits of this vehicle</u>. In your brochure, include a picture of the car and details about how it works
       (Topic)
compared to traditional cars.

- -

Scientific Achievements

NAS STANDARD: Develop understanding of science and technology in society

R.A.F.T.S. PROMPT FILLED-IN GRID:

Role: chairperson of the nomination committee
Audience: other committee members
Format: report
Topic: top three candidates for the award
Strong Verbs: select and explain

R.A.F.T.S. PROMPT IN PARAGRAPH FORM:

You are the <u>chairperson of the nomination committee</u> of an international organization that awards
(Role)

prizes to the creators of scientific innovations that benefit society. <u>Select</u> <u>your top three candidates</u>
(Strong verb)   **(Topic)**

<u>for this award</u> and <u>explain</u> the reasons for your choices in a <u>report</u> to <u>other committee members</u>.
(Strong verb)   **(Format)**   **(Audience)**

A vote of all the committee members will determine the nominees who receive the award.

> **Science—Science in Personal and Social Perspectives**
>
> Copy and distribute the reproducible R.A.F.T.S. prompts for *Exercise and Health*, *Maintaining Water Reserves*, *Protecting Your Local Environment*, *Marketing a New Car*, and *Scientific Achievements* on pages 76–77 or create additional R.A.F.T.S. prompts by using the blank grid found on page 79.

History and Nature of Science

Interactive Science Exhibits

NAS STANDARD: Develop understanding of science as a human endeavor

R.A.F.T.S. PROMPT FILLED-IN GRID:

Role: ticket seller at a museum
Audience: visitors
Format: brochure
Topic: the different interactive exhibits
Strong Verb: highlight

R.A.F.T.S. PROMPT IN PARAGRAPH FORM:

You are a <u>ticket seller at a museum</u> of science and industry. Create a <u>brochure</u> to hand to <u>visitors</u>
(Role)   **(Format)**   **(Audience)**

as they enter the museum <u>highlighting</u> <u>the different interactive exhibits</u> available for them to view
(Strong verb)   **(Topic)**

and enjoy.

Invention That Changed the World

NAS STANDARD: Develop understandings of the nature of science

R.A.F.T.S. PROMPT FILLED-IN GRID:

Role: inventor
Audience: yourself
Format: diary
Topic: impact your invention has had on today's world
Strong Verb: ponder

R.A.F.T.S. PROMPT IN PARAGRAPH FORM:

You are the <u>inventor</u> of the computer, the automobile, the telephone, or another major piece of
          (Role/Audience)
technology. In a <u>journal entry</u>, <u>ponder</u> the enormous <u>impact your invention</u> has had on today's
               (Format)   (Strong verb)   (Topic)
world. You may want to include pictures of what the invention looked like in its early stages of

development compared to how it looks today.

Scientist for All Time

NAS STANDARD: Develop understanding of the history of science

R.A.F.T.S. PROMPT FILLED-IN GRID:

Role: you
Audience: scientist in the past
Format: questions and answers
Topic: greatest contribution to science
Strong Verbs: write and record

R.A.F.T.S. PROMPT IN PARAGRAPH FORM:

<u>You</u> are traveling backwards in a time machine. Select a date and place to meet the person who, in
(Role)
your opinion, has made the <u>greatest contribution to science</u>. <u>Write</u> the <u>questions</u> you will ask this
                          (Topic)   (Strong verb) (Format)
<u>scientist</u> and <u>record</u> the <u>answers</u> so that you can update library reference materials when you return
(Audience)   (Strong verb)   (Format)
to the present.

> ### Science—History and Nature of Science
>
> Copy and distribute the reproducible R.A.F.T.S. prompts for *Interactive Science Exhibits, Invention That Changed the World,* and *Scientist for All Time* on page 77 or create additional R.A.F.T.S. prompts by using the blank grid found on page 79.

Math

NUMBER AND OPERATIONS

Restaurant Dilemma

You are eating out with your family at a local restaurant. You order three hamburgers with French fries at

$6.59 each, one chicken salad at $8.49, two iced teas at $1.39 each, three sodas at $1.39 each, and six

desserts at $3.99 each. But when you receive your bill, you realize you've been charged for an extra soda

and two extra desserts. Revise your bill to get an accurate total. Then write a comment card to the
(Strong verb)   **(Topic)**   **(Format)**

manager, expressing your concern that you have been overcharged and show how you corrected the error.
(Audience) (Strong verb)   **(Role)**

- -

Field Trip Preparation

You are the supervisor of transportation for a local school district. Write an e-mail to a teacher who needs to know
     (Role)   **(Format)**   **(Audience)**

how much it will cost to take a field trip to the art museum, which is 20 miles away. In your message, explain the
(Topic)   **(Strong verb)**

cost of transportation, knowing that the bus you plan to use gets nine miles per gallon of gasoline, and the going

rate for gasoline these days is $1.59 per gallon.

- -

Math Problem for All

You are a top math student and your teacher has asked you to help your classmates with a math problem.
     (Role)   **(Audience)**

Create an overhead transparency to demonstrate how you would solve the problem 56 x 22. Be sure you
(Strong verb)   **(Format)**   **(Topic)**

include each step in your process so that your classmates will understand how you came up with the

correct answer.

- -

ALGEBRA

Real-Life Algebra

Your teacher has introduced your class to algebra and has stressed how useful it will be in life. Write a
(Audience)

journal entry contemplating how algebra will help you solve everyday math problems and whether you are
(Format)   **(Strong verb)**   **(Topic)**   **(Role)**

sold on the idea or think it is just going to make things more confusing.

- -

"Believe It or Not" Algebra Formula

You are a math student who keeps a "Believe It or Not" journal filled with fascinating mathematical
(Audience)   **(Role)**   **(Format)**

information. The latest entry is the longest algebraic formula that can be solved. Write about this discovery,
     (Topic)

explain where you found it and describe how it was originally used.
(Strong verb)

Game Night

You are a parent planning a school "game night" and have obtained from the city fire chief the formula for
(Role)

determining maximum room capacity. Apply the formula he provided to the dimensions of the gym to

calculate how many people can attend game night. Then write a letter to the school principal including this
(Strong verb)   (Topic)   (Format)   (Audience)

information so he'll approve your request to use the gym for this function.

- -

Payday Payoff

You are the payroll clerk for the local department store. Your supervisor has just approved a five percent cost-
(Role)

of-living raise for all employees, effective immediately. Write a memo to employees explaining how much of
(Format)   (Audience) (Strong verb)

an increase they can expect in their paychecks in terms of dollars.
(Topic)

- -

GEOMETRY

Geometric Homes

Geometric Homes, a cutting-edge architecture firm, bases all of its designs on geometric shapes. As its

head architect, you are asked to design an advertisement for the president of Geometric Homes to review,
(Role)   (Strong verb) (Format)   (Audience)

showcasing four new homes. In your advertisement, include appropriate names and descriptions for each one.
(Topic)

- -

Backyard Grids

Your dog has dug holes in the backyard and your dad is afraid he will step in them as he mows the lawn.

You think you know how you can help. Create a grid of the backyard for your dad, pointing out the exact
(Role)   (Format)   (Audience)   (Strong verb)

location of each of the holes in order to avoid mishaps.
(Topic)

- -

Baseball Field

As part of a student group in your math class, you are working on plans for a new baseball field. Create a
(Role)   (Strong verb)

final design plan and cover letter to submit to the local school committee for approval of the plan, to make
(Format)   (Format)   (Audience)   (Topic)

sure it meets regulations.

- -

Puzzle Design

You are a toy designer who works in the puzzle department of Ricardo's Toy Company. The sales team has
(Role)

reported to you that kids really like colorful puzzles in geometric shapes. Design a puzzle with this in mind,
(Audience)   (Topic)   (Strong verb) (Format)

fashioning it so that all the pieces interlock. Give your puzzle a catchy name and include a few simple
(Strong verb)   (Format)

instructions on how to assemble it.

- -

MEASUREMENT

Kilometers to Miles

Your father just bought a new European car with an odometer that shows distance in kilometers, not miles.

Since this might take getting used to for you, your parents, and siblings, generate step-by-step instructions
(Role)   (Strong verb)   (Format)

that your family can use for converting kilometers to miles.
(Audience)   (Topic)

Writing to Promote in the Trait-Based Classroom: Content Areas Scholastic Teaching Resources

Substitute Schedules

Your teacher is taking a day off to attend a conference and has asked the class to <u>create</u> a daily schedule for
(Strong verb)
<u>the substitute</u>. <u>You and your classmates</u> decide to write <u>two schedules broken down into fifteen-minute time</u>
  (Audience)   **(Role)**   **(Format)**
<u>periods: 1) the typical everyday schedule and 2) the schedule of your dream day at school</u>.
                                     (Topic)

- -

DATA ANALYSIS AND PROBABILITY

Lunch Menus

Your classmates are interested in changing the school lunch menus and have selected you as their <u>spokesperson</u>.
                                                           (Role)
After surveying the student body to collect information about healthy yet tasty meals, write a <u>letter</u> to <u>the school</u>
                                                        (Format)   **(Audience)**
<u>lunch officials</u>, <u>arguing</u> for <u>new meals</u> students would enjoy. Include the data you collected in your letter to help
        (Strong verb)   **(Topic)**
build your case.

- -

Perennial Growth

You are a botanist's <u>lab assistant</u>. For the past few weeks, you have been collecting data on the <u>growth cycle</u>
              (Role)   **(Topic)**
<u>of perennial flowers</u> during their first three years of life. Now you are ready to share your findings with <u>your</u>
                                                                   (Audience)
<u>boss</u>. <u>Prepare</u> a <u>final report</u> with charts, tables, or graphs that best display the information you have collected.
  (Strong verb)   **(Format)**

- -

Baseball Fame

You are a <u>high school baseball player</u>. A <u>sports card company executive</u> is interested in putting your photo
               (Role)   **(Audience)**
and statistics on a baseball card as part of a series focusing on young players. At the executive's request,

<u>predict</u> your <u>home runs, batting average, and runs batted in for the forthcoming year</u> based on your
(Strong verb)   **(Topic)**
performance from past seasons, and send the information to him in an <u>e-mail</u>.
                                                       (Format)

- -

Friday Night at the Movies

One of your favorite things to do is go to the movies with your friends on Friday nights. However, this week

one of your teachers called to inform your parents that you haven't been doing your homework. <u>Create</u> the
                                                               (Strong verb)
<u>script of a phone conversation</u> between <u>you</u> and <u>one of your friends</u>, discussing the <u>probability of your</u>
    (Format)   **(Role)**   **(Audience)**
<u>parents letting you go to the movies</u> this week.
           (Topic)

- -

PROBLEM SOLVING

Math Game

<u>One of your friends</u> is having a hard time understanding math operations. So it's up to <u>you</u> to <u>create</u>
  (Audience)   **(Role)** **(Strong verb)**
<u>ten game cards</u>, each with an <u>everyday math problem</u>. On the back of each card, record the best operation to
 (Format)   **(Topic)**
solve the problem. For example, if the problem for the front of the card reads, "If I received 23 e-mails each day

for a week, how many e-mails do I get by the end of the week?" the answer on the back should be

"multiplication."

Writing to Prompts in the Trait-Based Classroom: Content Areas · Scholastic Teaching Resources

Recipe Remedy

Your mother has agreed to help you bake your favorite pie. As a <u>pie-loving son or daughter</u>, <u>take the original</u>
(Role)
<u>recipe for one pie and triple it</u> so that there is enough pie for everyone in the family. <u>Record</u> the <u>new recipe</u> so
(Topic)   **(Strong verb)**   **(Format)**
that <u>you and your mom</u> can start baking.
(Audience)

The Challenge of 10

<u>You and a small group of classmates</u> have been given the challenge to come up with as many <u>problems</u> as
(Role)   **(Topic)**
possible <u>with the answer "10."</u> You can use fractions, decimals, number patterns—whatever makes sense.
(Topic)
Once your group has created a <u>list</u> of problems, <u>compare</u> it with the other groups' lists and <u>make</u> a <u>chart</u> for
                                   (Strong verb)   **(Strong verb)**   **(Format)**
the <u>whole class</u> of all the possibilities.
(Audience)

Doghouse

<u>You</u> are building a new doghouse for your puppy. You have a design that will fit the puppy perfectly now.
(Role/Audience)
However, you realize that he will grow and, therefore, you need to accommodate his maximum size. Estimate
how large you think your puppy will become, figure out <u>the dimensions of the new doghouse</u>, and <u>create</u> a
                                                        (Topic)   **(Strong verb)**
<u>revised design</u>.
(Format)

REASONING AND PROOF

Everyday Math

You are a <u>math tutor</u> at a local elementary school. You have been asked by the teachers to help <u>students</u>
       (Role)   **(Audience)**
understand the importance of mathematics by connecting math to real-life situations. <u>Think</u> of two examples
                                                           (Strong verb)
where <u>multiplication is used in everyday life</u> and <u>write</u> them out in a <u>story problem</u> for your students to solve in
                   (Topic)   **(Strong verb)**   **(Format)**
tutoring sessions.

Rows of Carrots

You are a <u>vegetable gardener</u> who is planning your spring crop of carrots. You know that if you plant one
       (Role/Audience)
row, you will get enough carrots for several family meals, but you would like more than that. <u>Figure</u> out
                                                                       (Strong verb)
<u>how many rows of carrots</u> you think you will need to keep your family fed for at least a month. <u>Write</u> out
(Topic)   **(Strong verb)**
your <u>plan</u> so that you know how many seeds to plant.
   (Format)

Math Discussion

<u>You</u> and your best friend are having a heated discussion about math. Your friend says there's no room for
(Role)
math in everyday life. You disagree. To convince your friend, make a <u>list</u> of <u>activities that might occur during</u>
                                                                   (Format)
<u>the day and in which math is needed,</u> such as grocery shopping or planning a building project. <u>Share</u> your list
(Topic)   **(Strong verb)**
with <u>your friend</u>. <u>Specify</u> the approach that is required to carry out each activity: addition, division, algebra,
    (Audience)   **(Strong verb)**
geometry, and so on.

Writing to Prompts in the Trait-Based Classroom: Content Areas · Scholastic Teaching Resources

Aquarium Troubles

<u>You</u> just went to a pet store and bought a used 20-gallon aquarium. After you get home, you get a
(Role)
gut-wrenching feeling that the tank will not hold that much water. <u>Design</u> a <u>plan</u> to determine <u>the amount of</u>
                                                                   (Strong verb) (Format)   (Topic)
<u>water your aquarium holds</u>. When it turns out that it really does hold less than 20 gallons, <u>write</u> a <u>letter</u> to
                                                                                               (Strong verb) (Format)
the <u>pet store owner</u> explaining how you determined that fact and <u>ask for a refund</u>.
    (Audience)   (Topic)

COMMUNICATION

Graphic Communication

<u>You</u> are expected to speak to <u>the class</u> about your graph or chart showing the <u>top ten most densely populated</u>
(Role)   (Audience)   (Topic)
<u>countries in the world</u>. In your <u>notes for your speech</u>, <u>explain</u> why you chose a particular chart or graph as the
                                   (Format)   (Strong verb)
best way to represent your data and the useful information you can glean from it.

Art and Mathematics

You are an experienced <u>artist</u> who is working with <u>young artists</u>. Today's lesson focuses on <u>how to draw human</u>
                       (Role)   (Audience)   (Topic)
<u>portraits based on photographs</u>. <u>Give</u> your protégés <u>step-by-step instructions</u> for measuring the face in the
                                    (Strong verb)   (Format)
photograph and determining the accurate proportions for enlarging it onto paper.

Math Mania

You are a <u>reporter</u> for the magazine *Math Mania*. For your next story, you plan to <u>interview</u> your son's math
          (Role)   (Audience)   (Strong verb)
teacher about <u>strategies she recommends for getting children interested in everyday math</u>, such as planning a
              (Topic)
garden, making change, or assembling a puzzle. Write the <u>list of questions</u> you plan to ask.
                                                          (Format)

Book Titles

You are a <u>children's book author</u> and <u>your publisher</u> has asked you to start thinking about writing a set of six
          (Role)   (Audience)
books about <u>math operations</u>—addition, subtraction, multiplication, division, algebra, and geometry. Write possible
            (Topic)
<u>titles with subtitles</u> for each book in order to catch a child's eye and <u>express</u> the operation precisely. For example,
(Format)   (Strong verb)
you might call the book on addition *The Sum of It All: Quirky Facts About Addition*.

CONNECTIONS

Temperature Control

You are a TV <u>meteorologist</u>. Each month, your report features the average daily temperature for the month. <u>Chart</u>
             (Role)   (Strong verb)
the <u>daily temperatures</u> on a graph to share with <u>viewers</u>, then write a <u>short introduction</u> for your report that
    (Topic)   (Audience)   (Format)
includes the average temperature.

Writing to Prompts in the Trait-Based Classroom: Content Areas Scholastic Teaching Resources

Average Scores for a Grade

<u>You</u> keep your weekly math grades in a notebook. This week your teacher asked you to <u>average your grades</u>
(Role) <u>to arrive at a median score</u> to <u>share</u> with your parents at a parent/teacher conference. Do this calculation,
      (Topic)   **(Strong verb)**
then <u>write</u> a <u>reflection</u> to share with <u>your parents</u> on how well you are succeeding in math.
(Strong verb)   **(Format)**   **(Audience)**

Math Autobiography

<u>You</u> have been asked by <u>your teacher</u> to keep a <u>mathematical autobiography</u>. <u>Document</u> for yourself the <u>first</u>
(Role)   **(Audience)**   **(Format)**   **(Strong verb)**
<u>time you remember using math to solve a problem outside of school</u>. Perhaps you were keeping score at a
      (Topic)
ball game or helping your parents figure out how much fabric to buy to cover a favorite old chair. Think back

to a time when you were glad you had math to solve a real-world problem.

REPRESENTATION

Desert Island

<u>You</u> were stranded on a deserted island. You had no calendar to <u>keep track of the days of the week or the</u>
(Role)   **(Topic)**
<u>months of the year</u>, so you used the sand and a stick to create <u>symbols</u>. Now that you have returned home,
      (Format)
<u>re-create</u> those symbols on paper so that you can share with <u>loved ones</u> how inventive you were.
(Strong verb)   **(Audience)**

Count Your Errors

<u>You</u> are giving a two-minute speech entitled "Principal for a Day." During a practice run, you ask a friend to
(Role)
count the number of times you pause, use "umm," or utter other short, distracting sounds. <u>Your friend</u> does
      (Audience)
this by making <u>tally marks</u> at <u>problem points</u> on a printed copy of the speech. Reread your speech from this
    (Format)   **(Topic)**
marked copy, <u>noting</u> the marks in the text and making efforts to improve your performance.
      (Strong verb)

Paper-Folding Contest

<u>You</u> and <u>your best friend</u> have entered into a contest to see <u>how many times a piece of paper can be folded</u>.
(Role)   **(Audience)**   **(Topic)**
You believe that a larger piece of paper can be folded more times than a smaller one. Your friend says that it

will be the same number of folds no matter what size the paper. Write down the <u>rules for your contest</u> and
      (Format)
then <u>proceed</u> to go through the steps to figure out who is correct.
  (Strong verb)

Social Studies

CULTURE

Travel Plans

As the <u>assistant to the president of the United States</u>, you are responsible for reviewing all nominees for the
(Role)
position of U.S. Ambassador to Mexico. Write the final <u>report</u> you give to <u>the president</u> for <u>your choice of the</u>
(Format) **(Audience)** **(Topic)**
<u>top candidate</u>, <u>summarizing</u> the reasons you think this person will do a good job based on his or her beliefs,
(Strong verb)
knowledge, values, and understanding of Mexican culture and traditions.

- -

American Culture

You are a <u>journalist</u> for a national magazine who has been assigned to write an article about the <u>five most</u>
(Role)
<u>important American cultural events of the 1980's</u>. Make a <u>list</u> of these events and write a short <u>paragraph</u>
(Topic) **(Format)** **(Format)**
<u>explaining</u> the importance of each one to submit to your <u>editor</u>.
(Strong verb) **(Audience)**

- -

TIME, CONTINUITY, AND CHANGE

Frontier Fantasy

A <u>producer of a local TV station</u> is running a contest to choose a family to star in a new reality program about life
(Audience)
in a frontier cabin for a month, in order to show what life was like in the nineteenth century. <u>You</u> decide to write
(Role)
a <u>contest-entry essay</u> to <u>impress</u> the producer with your <u>knowledge of frontier life</u>. Good luck!
(Format) **(Strong verb)** **(Topic)**

- -

Changes

You are a <u>grandparent</u> who was born in the 1930's. When you were young, you shopped at a country store.
(Role)
As you got older, you shopped in supermarkets and department stores. Now you are shopping on the

Internet. Write a <u>letter</u> to your <u>grandchildren</u>, <u>describing</u> <u>the changes that have taken place over time</u> in the
(Format) **(Audience)** **(Strong verb)** **(Topic)**
way you buy things.

- -

PEOPLE, PLACES, AND ENVIRONMENTS

Places

You are the <u>author of a new guidebook</u> for <u>hikers</u> that <u>suggests</u> places to go hiking. Write <u>descriptions</u> of the
(Role) **(Audience)** **(Strong verb)** **(Format)**
<u>top three destinations</u> that you highly <u>recommend</u>.
(Topic) **(Strong verb)**

- -

Environments

You are a <u>member of the science team for Biosphere 10</u>. You will be living inside the biosphere for the next
(Role)
two years and have to wear only the clothes you packed and eat only the food you can produce. You forgot one

essential article of clothing, however. Write an <u>e-mail</u> to a <u>family member</u>, <u>pleading</u> with him or her to
(Format) **(Audience)** **(Strong verb)**
<u>send this important item</u> to you as soon as possible.
(Topic)

Writing to Prompts in the Trait-Based Classroom: Content Areas   Scholastic Teaching Resources

INDIVIDUAL DEVELOPMENT AND IDENTITY

Identity Role

You are a <u>candidate for governor</u> of your state, and a correspondent from the local television station is going
(Role)
to interview you. Write the <u>questions and answers</u> that will allow <u>viewers</u> to find <u>how you feel about an</u>
(Format) **(Audience)** **(Topic)**
<u>important campaign issue</u>, <u>revealing</u> who you are and what you stand for.
(Strong verb)

- -

License Plate

You are a <u>teenager</u> who has earned the money for your first car and you want to get <u>personalized license</u>
(Role) **(Format)**
<u>plates</u>. Design several possible license plate letter and number combinations that <u>convey your distinct</u>
(Strong verb) **(Topic)**
<u>personality</u> to <u>other drivers</u>.
(Audience)

- -

INDIVIDUALS, GROUPS, AND INSTITUTIONS

Library Policy

As a student at your school, <u>you</u> just found out that your <u>favorite book has been banned from the school</u>
(Role) **(Topic)**
<u>library</u>. You decide to call a meeting of <u>other students</u> who might be as concerned as you are about this
(Audience)
possibility. <u>Develop</u> the <u>poster</u> you will hang up in public areas, announcing the meeting.
(Strong verb) **(Format)**

- -

Dress Code

You are the <u>student representative</u> for the local school committee. Some of the members would like to
(Role)
change the <u>school dress code to uniforms</u>. Write a <u>questionnaire</u> to be administered to
(Topic) **(Format)**
<u>the student body, parents, teachers, and administrators</u> to <u>gather</u> information about how each group feels
(Audience) **(Strong verb)**
about this proposed policy.

- -

POWER, AUTHORITY, AND GOVERNANCE

Adopt-a-Park Campaign

You are the <u>student liaison</u> to the City Parks and Recreation Bureau. You find out that a <u>park near your school</u>
(Role) **(Topic)**
<u>is going to be closing</u> because it costs too much to maintain. However, if you can <u>appeal</u> to your fellow
(Strong verb)
<u>classmates</u> to join the "Adopt-a-Park" program, there is a good chance the park can stay open. <u>Design</u> the
(Audience) **(Strong verb)**
<u>campaign</u> to save your park, which consists of a poster, a bumper sticker, and a lapel button.
(Format)

- -

Group Conflict Resolution

Your soccer team has been invited to an <u>out-of-town tournament that takes place over Thanksgiving</u>. Some of
(Topic)
the parents don't want their children to go, but <u>you</u> need everyone on the team to be there if you stand any
(Role)
chance of winning. Develop a strongly worded <u>position paper</u> to <u>convince</u> those <u>parents</u> to change their
(Format) **(Strong verb)** **(Audience)**
minds.

PRODUCTION, DISTRIBUTION, AND CONSUMPTION

Public Notice

You are the <u>head of marketing</u> for a company that manufactures computer games. You just found out there is
(Role)
a <u>virus in one of your games</u>. Write the <u>recall notice</u> you send to the <u>president of the company that</u>
(Topic)   (Format)   (Audience)
<u>distributes the game</u>, <u>explaining</u> the problem and how you plan to rectify it.
                          (Strong verb)

Book Demand

The newest book in your favorite fantasy-fiction series is finally at the bookstore. When <u>you</u> get there,
                                                                                        (Role)
the manager tells you she is sold out and can't get more copies anytime soon. Write a <u>letter</u> to the
                                                                                      (Format)
<u>publisher</u> <u>expressing</u> your disappointment in <u>not being able to get a copy of the new book</u>. In your letter,
(Audience) (Strong verb)   (Topic)
suggest ways to avoid shortages in the future.

SCIENCE, TECHNOLOGY, AND SOCIETY

New Technology

You are a <u>technical writer</u> who has been hired by an inventor to write an <u>easy-to-understand instructional</u>
          (Role)   (Format)
<u>manual</u> for a new robot that every family will want because it can cook everyone's favorite meals. Your

manual should <u>inform</u> <u>families</u> of <u>how to operate the robot</u>.
              (Strong verb) (Audience)   (Topic)

Space Debate

Ever since the American public watched the televised moon landing in 1969, people have been arguing

about <u>whether Neil Armstrong actually landed on the moon or whether he was part of a technology hoax</u>.
                                                (Topic)
NASA has put together a scientific research panel to put this issue to rest for once and for all. As a

<u>member of the panel</u>, write the <u>notes</u> that you will <u>present</u> to the <u>other members</u> to <u>support</u> your position
(Role)   (Format)   (Strong verb)   (Audience)   (Strong verb)
that the moon landing was real.

GLOBAL CONNECTIONS

Human Rights

You are a <u>United States senator</u> who is concerned that housing is too costly for many of the <u>citizens</u> of
          (Role)   (Audience)
your state. Write the <u>brief statement</u> that comes at the beginning of a law you are <u>proposing</u> that calls for
                       (Format)   (Strong verb)
<u>new taxes being spent on building affordable housing</u>.
                      (Topic)

Environmental Greetings

<u>You</u> and your classmates are creating <u>greeting cards</u> that you will sell during National Wildlife Week to <u>raise</u>
(Role)   (Format)
<u>money for the local animal shelter</u>. The cards feature photographs of local wildlife. <u>Create</u> the text for the
           (Topic)   (Strong verb)
cards that will appeal to <u>parents and other members of the community</u>.
                          (Audience)

CIVIC IDEALS AND PRACTICES

Civic-Minded

You are a <u>filmmaker</u> creating a documentary about a <u>local philanthropist</u> who has done a lot of good for your
      (Role)   (Topic)
<u>community</u>. Write the <u>narration</u> for the opening of the film that will <u>highlight</u> her many civic-minded
(Audience)   (Format)   (Strong verb)
contributions.

Influential Citizen

While studying U.S. geography, <u>you</u> realize that one state, our capital city, and towns in every state have been
                    (Role)
named after George Washington. <u>You and your teacher</u> decide to research <u>things George Washington</u>
                           (Audience)   (Topic)
<u>accomplished in his lifetime</u>, in addition to being the first President. <u>Compile</u> a <u>list</u> of the top five contributions
                                                 (Strong verb) (Format)
you discover.

Science

SCIENCE AS INQUIRY

Scientific Inquiry in Action

You are a <u>marine life researcher</u> and have been asked to <u>compile</u> information on <u>poisonous fish found in the</u>
        (Role)   (Strong verb)   (Topic)
<u>oceans of the world</u> for <u>visitors to your organization's Web site</u>. Write a <u>plan</u> describing the steps you will take
                        (Audience)   (Format)
to find this information, carry out that plan, and <u>create</u> a <u>list</u> of the fish you locate.
                                    (Strong verb) (Format)

Funding Scientific Research

You are a <u>research scientist</u> who is working on an important project to discover cures for communicable
        (Role)
diseases. Your work requires special equipment that is very expensive. Write a <u>fundraising letter</u> to send to
                                                          (Format)
<u>prospective donors</u>, <u>persuading</u> them to <u>contribute money for the equipment</u>.
    (Audience)   (Strong verb)   (Topic)

PHYSICAL SCIENCE

Hardness of Minerals

In science, <u>you</u> learn about common minerals and their uses. <u>Create</u> a <u>poster with captions</u> for your
         (Role)   (Strong verb)   (Format)
<u>classmates</u> that shows <u>the hardness of five minerals and where they are commonly found</u>.
(Audience)   (Topic)

Motion and Forces in Racing

As a <u>race car driver</u> who has just won your first race, write an <u>article</u> for <u>readers of *Racing Enthusiast's*</u>
    (Role)   (Format)   (Audience)
Monthly <u>expressing</u> how your <u>car's frictionless body style helped</u> lead you to victory. Be sure to thank your car
(Strong verb)   (Topic)
designer and your sponsors for their support in making it all possible.

Writing to Promote in the Trait-Based Classroom: Content Areas · Scholastic Teaching Resources

Energy that Keeps You Warm

You are the <u>tour director</u> for a group of <u>students</u> who are traveling through the United States over winter
    (Role)   (Audience)
break. <u>Create</u> a <u>list</u> of <u>types of clothing</u> they will need for stops in Florida, Maine, California, and Minnesota
   (Strong verb) (Format)   (Topic)
so that they will know exactly what to pack. Give examples of items of clothing you recommend and explain

why you recommend them.

- -

LIFE SCIENCE

The Functions of Human Organs

You are the <u>brain</u> in a human body and you notice that some organs are not working well to keep the body
    (Role)
functioning. Write a <u>pep talk</u> to give to <u>the organs,</u> <u>encouraging</u> them to <u>keep digestion, respiration, and</u>
   (Format)   (Audience) (Strong verb)   (Topic)
<u>circulation in tip-top shape</u>. Be sure to include sound reasoning for your concerns.

- -

Learning about Heredity

<u>You</u> have been looking through family albums and notice you have some <u>physical characteristics that you</u>
(Role)   (Topic)
<u>inherited from past generations</u>. Your height, hair color, and the shape of your nose, and even your build match

those of relatives from both sides of your family. <u>Make</u> a <u>list</u> of these characteristics and <u>describe</u> them in detail
                                             (Strong verb) (Format)   (Strong verb)
so that you can share the list with <u>family members</u> at an upcoming reunion.
                                (Audience)

- -

Behavior and Care of Animals

You are a <u>pet store owner</u> and have just hired a new clerk to care for the animals while you're on vacation.
        (Role)
Write a <u>set of instructions</u> for the <u>clerk,</u> <u>explaining</u> <u>how to keep an animal of your choice healthy and happy</u>.
   (Format)   (Audience) (Strong verb)   (Topic)

- -

Ecosystem Skits

You are the <u>head of the local garden club</u> and have been asked by a <u>second-grade teacher</u> to create a fun
         (Role)   (Audience)
way to help students learn about ecosystems. Write a <u>short skit</u> for <u>her students</u> to perform that has parts for
                                               (Format)   (Audience)
producers, consumers, and decomposers, and that <u>demonstrates</u> <u>how these roles work in an garden</u>
                                        (Strong verb)   (Topic)
<u>ecosystem</u>.

- -

Discovery of New Life Form

As an avid <u>scuba diver,</u> you think you might have <u>discovered a new species of fish</u> that lives in shallow water.
        (Role)   (Topic)
Write a <u>letter</u> to a <u>marine biologist</u> at the local university <u>inquiring</u> if she might be interested in investigating your
   (Format)   (Audience)   (Strong verb)
discovery. Include a detailed observation of how this new species adapts to its environment, your detailed

observations of the species, and what you'd like to name it.

- -

EARTH AND SPACE SCIENCE

The Water Cycle

You are a single <u>drop of ocean water</u> that is beginning a trip through <u>the water cycle</u>. Write an imaginative
            (Role and Audience)   (Topic)
<u>trip log</u> to <u>record</u> your progress as you evaporate from the ocean, travel through the air, rain down on the
(Format) (Strong verb)
land, and flow back to the ocean.

Writing to Prompts in the Trait-Based Classroom: Content Areas *Scholastic Teaching Resources*

Earthquake Alert

You are a <u>geologist</u> who studies the movement of the plates that make up the Earth's crust.
(Role)
Write a <u>TV commentary</u> you might deliver to <u>people living on or near fault lines</u>, <u>alerting</u> them to
(Format)   (Audience)   (Strong verb)
<u>the dangers of earthquakes and their history in your region.</u>
(Topic)

- -

New Planet Discovery

You are a <u>renowned astronomer</u> who has documented many comets and asteroids. Now, you have
(Role)
discovered something even more exciting: <u>a new planet in orbit around the sun.</u> Write an <u>announcement</u> for
(Topic)   (Format)
the <u>leaders of the scientific community</u>, <u>proclaiming</u> your discovery. Include specific details from your notes to
(Audience)   (Strong verb)
authenticate your claim.

- -

SCIENCE AND TECHNOLOGY

Technology for Household Help

<u>You</u> have entered a contest to design a <u>machine that will clean your room.</u> Draw a <u>picture</u> of your machine
(Role)   (Topic)   (Format)
with <u>captions</u> that <u>explain</u> how it works. If you win the contest, the <u>team of engineers</u> will build your machine.
(Format)   (Strong verb)   (Audience)

- -

Designing for Market

You are an <u>organic farmer</u> who has perfected a new way to grow more nutritious and delicious tomatoes. In
(Role)
an <u>e-mail</u>, ask your <u>delivery company manager</u> to <u>design</u> a <u>new container that will get your tomatoes to</u>
(Format)   (Audience)   (Strong verb)   (Topic)
<u>market without bruising.</u> Be sure to give all the information he needs to create a proposal: the average size of

the tomatoes, how far they will travel, and how long they need to stay in the containers before they are sold.

- -

SCIENCE IN PERSONAL AND SOCIAL PERSPECTIVES

Exercise and Health

Radio station KBY has scheduled a three-minute debate for <u>listeners</u> between an <u>exercise guru and a couch</u>
(Audience)   (Role)
potato. Write the <u>debate</u> <u>arguing</u> the <u>pros and cons of daily exercise.</u> Include information that grounds each
(Format) (Strong verb)   (Topic)
argument in facts affecting health.

- -

Maintaining Water Reserves

As a <u>concerned citizen</u>, write a <u>letter</u> to the <u>city planner</u> <u>alerting</u> him to the fact that the one and only <u>water</u>
(Role)   (Format)   (Audience)   (Strong verb)
<u>reservoir isn't large enough to supply all the new houses that are being built.</u> In your letter, include some
(Topic)
alternative ways of supplying water to local homeowners and businesses.

- -

Protecting Your Local Environment

You are a <u>new resident</u> in town and have just learned that the waste disposal committee is planning to build
(Role)
a landfill near your house. <u>Create</u> a <u>petition</u> for your <u>neighbors</u> to sign that informs them and <u>the committee</u>
(Strong verb)   (Format)   (Audience)   (Audience)
of <u>the environmental hazards of a landfill</u>, specifically that chemicals would leach into the local water supply.
(Topic)

Writing to Prompts in the Trait-Based Classroom: Content Areas Scholastic Teaching Resources

Marketing a New Car

You are the <u>marketing executive of an automobile manufacturer</u> that is offering a revolutionary
             (Role)
new car that runs half on gas and half on electricity. <u>Design</u> a <u>brochure</u> informing <u>buyers</u> of the
                           (Strong verb)   **(Format)**   **(Audience)**
<u>benefits of this vehicle</u>. In your brochure, include a picture of the car and details about how it works
     (Topic)
compared to traditional cars.

- -

Scientific Achievements

You are the <u>chairperson of the nomination committee</u> of an international organization that awards prizes to
                    (Role)
the creators of scientific innovations that benefit society. <u>Select</u> <u>your top three candidates for this award</u> and
                         (Strong verb)   **(Topic)**
<u>explain</u> the reasons for your choices in a <u>report</u> to <u>other committee members</u>. A vote of all the committee
(Strong verb)   **(Format)**   **(Audience)**
members will determine the nominees who receive the award.

- -

HISTORY AND NATURE OF SCIENCE

Interactive Science Exhibits

You are a <u>ticket seller at a museum</u> of science and industry. Create a <u>brochure</u> to hand to <u>visitors</u> as they
        (Role)   **(Format)**   **(Audience)**
enter the museum <u>highlighting</u> <u>the different interactive exhibits</u> available for them to view and enjoy.
             (Strong verb)   **(Topic)**

- -

Invention That Changed the World

You are the <u>inventor</u> of the computer, the automobile, the telephone, or another major piece of technology.
     (Role/Audience)
In a <u>journal entry</u>, <u>ponder</u> the enormous <u>impact your invention</u> has had on today's world. You may want to
    (Format)   **(Strong verb)**   **(Topic)**
include pictures of what the invention looked like in its early stages of development compared to how it

looks today.

- -

Scientist for All Time

<u>You</u> are traveling backwards in a time machine. Select a date and place to meet the person who, in your
(Role)
opinion, has made the <u>greatest contribution to science</u>. <u>Write</u> the <u>questions</u> you will ask this <u>scientist</u> and
               (Topic)   **(Strong verb)**   **(Format)**   **(Audience)**
<u>record</u> the <u>answers</u> so that you can update library reference materials when you return to the present.
(Strong verb) (Format)

- -

Creating Your Own R.A.F.T.S. Prompts

After successfully using the ready-to-use R.A.F.T.S. prompts, you may wish to create your own based on what you're covering in the content areas. Let's say your students are working on how multiplication might be used on a daily basis in real-life situations. Using the blank reproducible grids on page 79, you might choose the following R.A.F.T.S. components:

Role:	owner of a window washing company
Audience:	school principal
Format:	proposal
Topic:	how much it will cost to wash all the windows in the school, how long it will take, and why your company deserves this contract
Strong Verb:	inform

Once you have completed the grid, take the five components and create a paragraph. Underline and label each component so that it is clear to students.

You are the owner of a <u>window washing company</u>. Write a
                                    (Role)
<u>proposal</u> for the <u>school principal</u> <u>informing</u> him of <u>how much</u>
  (Format)   **(Audience)**   **(Strong verb)**
<u>it will cost to wash all the windows in the school</u>, how long it
                        (Topic)
will take, and why you your company deserves this contract.

Then, write your R.A.F.T.S. paragraph on the board or make photocopies—and have students start thinking about what they will write. As students begin to write, remind them to think about the relationship between each component and the traits of writing. For example, with this defined **R**ole, students write not as themselves, but as the owner of a window washing company. They must write for a specific **A**udience, the school principal, and therefore say what needs to be said not only using appropriate **voice**, but also interesting **word choices**. Because you give them a defined **F**ormat, a proposal, your students must also focus their attention on the organization of the writing. (See page 80 for an extensive list of formats.) The **T**opic is inspired by ideas you are studying in math, science, and social studies. Lastly, with a **S**trong verb, students must motivate their audience with creative **ideas**, effective **organization**, appropriate **voice**, interesting **word choice**, smooth **sentence fluency**, and correct **conventions**. (See page 80 for an extensive list of strong verbs.) It's easy to see how R.A.F.T.S. prompts and writing traits go hand-in-hand to help your students focus their writing for success.

Reproducible Blank R.A.F.T.S. Grids

- -

SUBJECT AREA: _____

ROLE: _____

AUDIENCE: _____

FORMAT: _____

TOPIC: _____

STRONG VERB: _____

- -

SUBJECT AREA: _____

ROLE: _____

AUDIENCE: _____

FORMAT: _____

TOPIC: _____

STRONG VERB: _____

- -

SUBJECT AREA: _____

ROLE: _____

AUDIENCE: _____

FORMAT: _____

TOPIC: _____

STRONG VERB: _____

FORMATS AND STRONG VERBS TO CONSIDER WHEN CREATING YOUR OWN PROMPTS

FORMATS

advertisement
anecdote
announcement
application
biographical sketch
blurb
board game
brochure
caption
commentary
contest entry form
consumer guide
critique
debate
"Dear Abby" letter
definition
dialogue
diary entry
dictionary entry
directions
discussion

editorial
e-mail
encyclopedia entry
epitaph
eulogy
free-verse poem
graffiti
greeting card
historical account
instructions
interview
introduction
journal entry
last will and testament
lecture
legislation
lesson plan
letter
letter to the editor
list
map
math problems

memo
menu
monologue
motivational speech
motto
newspaper article
note
oration
package copy
parody
personalized license
    plates
poem
post card
poster
prediction
prophecy
puzzle
rebuttal
reflection
request
résumé

review
screenplay
sermon
ship's log
short story
skit
slogan
song
speech
stream of
    consciousness
summary
survival manual
telegram
telephone dialogue
test questions
thumbnail sketch
top-ten list
travel log
"Wanted" poster
word puzzle

STRONG VERBS

align
amaze
analyze
announce
annoy
apply
assimilate
brainstorm
browse
capture
carve
censor
characterize
charge
clarify
coalesce
combine
communicate
compare
connect

connive
consider
construct
contemplate
create
critique
decipher
defend
define
describe
determine
diagnose
divulge
edit
embellish
empathize
encourage
engrave
examine
exemplify
explain

explore
express
extol
highlight
illuminate
imagine
improvise
inform
inspect
investigate
memorize
mold
motivate
outline
participate
persuade
photograph
predict
quote
realize
reconcile

reconstruct
record
reflect
reject
relate
remind
review
script
scrutinize
search
showcase
specify
summarize
suppress
trigger
understand
urge
visualize
warn